The Evidence-Based Investor

Pascal Böni · Tim Kröncke

The Evidence-Based Investor

Overcoming Investment Myths for Better Performance

palgrave
macmillan

Pascal Böni
Tilburg School of Economics
and Management & TIAS
Tilburg University
Tilburg, The Netherlands

Tim Kröncke
School of Business
FHNW University of Applied Sciences
and Arts Northwestern Switzerland
Basel, Switzerland

ISBN 978-3-031-88674-4 ISBN 978-3-031-88675-1 (eBook)
https://doi.org/10.1007/978-3-031-88675-1

This work was supported by Remaco Asset Management AG.

Cover credit: Image by Triff

This Palgrave Macmillan imprint is published by the registered company Springer Nature Switzerland AG
The registered company address is: Gewerbestrasse 11, 6330 Cham, Switzerland

About This Book

Investing is simple in theory, yet difficult in practice. Investors give up return and often unknowingly increase risk by falling for one or more of the investment myths which we expose in this book. We explore why countless investors keep falling into the same traps, warn against the alluring, though deceptive voices of the investment world, and unravel ten specific myths that often lead investors astray. To avoid these pitfalls, a scientifically based and disciplined approach to investing is presented, one which is centred around only three sub-portfolios. Based on empirical and theoretical insights, this book empowers readers to make smarter, better-informed investment decisions. If you want to master the art of investing and build a prosperous financial future, this book will serve as your essential guide.

Contents

About the Authors

Pascal Böni is Professor of Practice in Finance and Private Markets at Tilburg School of Economics and Management, and Associate Professor of Finance at TIAS School for Business and Society, Tilburg University, The Netherlands. He heads the Tilburg Institute for Private Markets (TiPM) and lectures Corporate Finance and Mergers & Acquisitions at TIAS, Tilburg University's business school. He is the academic director of the MBA in Finance/ Master in Finance—Program of the Universities of Basel and Tilburg. His main research interests are in private markets. His work has been published in academic journals, various trade journals, and books. He is a regular speaker at national and international academic and industry conferences.

Furthermore, he is the CEO of Remaco Group, a Swiss financial advisory company belonging to Nexia International, a leading global network of independent accounting and consulting firms. He serves or has served on the board of directors of several companies, for example, the board of directors of the Swiss Association of Securities Firms (SASF), as well as the board of various listed and unlisted national and international companies in the media, the energy, the IT, and the financial services industry. He advised some 100+ corporate finance and M&A transactions. Previously, he worked in management consulting, for leading firms such as Groupe BPI, Paris, and Roland Berger & Partner, Munich. Pascal holds a Ph.D. in Finance from Tilburg University, a Master of Business Administration (MBA) from the University of Rochester, and a Master of Business Law (MBL) from the University of St. Gallen.

Tim Kröncke is Professor of Finance and Head of the Institute for Finance at the FHNW School of Business at the University of Applied Sciences and Arts Northwestern Switzerland. He is a capital markets enthusiast who has published in leading academic journals, such as the Journal of Finance, Journal of Financial Economics, and the Journal of Monetary Economics, and has participated in numerous practical research projects with government institutions and industry.

Furthermore, he is Chief Investment Officer at Remaco Asset Management AG. Previously, he was a Full Professor of Finance at the University of Neuchâtel, an Assistant Professor at the University of Basel, and a researcher at ZEW in Mannheim. He holds a Ph.D. in Finance from the University of Mannheim, a diploma in Economics from the University of Freiburg, and is a certified banker (IHK, Germany).

List of Figures

List of Tables

1

Prologue

We start from the observation that many investors do not actually have portfolios that are well aligned with what scientific research has suggested over the past few decades. Instead, investors get caught up in investing myths. The situation is reminiscent of the saga of Homer's Odysseus, where many sailors went shipwrecked by following the beautiful chants of the sirens. We propose a solution lending from the wisdom of Odysseus. By adopting an easy-to-implement, evidence-based approach, investors keep the course and can avoid falling for investment myths and financial shipwreck.

Myths are narratives transmitted through generations, "explaining" the origins and reasons behind various phenomena. In the world of investing, a discipline flooded with numbers, narratives are essential in shaping our perception of the world and justifying investment approaches. The latter have emerged over time and have come to be widely accepted, influencing the investment behaviours of millions of retail and professional investors alike. But are these narratives that underpin investment decisions really in the best interests of investors?

The first aim of this book is to show that many well-known investment narratives lack a sound economic rationale and even contradict the scientific literature on how investors should invest to achieve long-term capital appreciation. Many brilliant researchers have worked over the past decades to figure out how investors can build, implement and manage efficient investment portfolios. This is indeed not trivial and involves a number

P. Böni and T. Kröncke, *The Evidence-Based Investor*,
https://doi.org/10.1007/978-3-031-88675-1_1

of complex issues.[1]The pertinent literature is not light in weight either. Within the Economic Sciences, research on investment decisions has regularly been selected to receive the Nobel Memorial Prize. Established in 1968 by Sweden's central bank, the Nobel Memorial Prize in Economic Sciences was awarded multiple times to researchers investigating investment topics. The list of laureates who have contributed to our knowledge of investing includes Samuelson (who recieved the Nobel Prize in 1970), Arrow (in 1972), Tobin (in 1981), Modigliani (in 1985), Markowitz (in 1990), Miller (in 1990), Sharpe (in 1990), Merton (in 1997), Scholes (in 1997), Kahneman (in 2002), Engle (in 2003), Fama (in 2013), Hansen (in 2013), Shiller (in 2013) and Thaler (in 2017).

Empirical studies show time and time again that the scientific approach to investing is indeed sound. The performance of many real-world investment portfolios would improve dramatically if only investors replaced a narrative-based approach by an evidence-based investment approach. In this book, we will expose the problems inherent in many investment narratives and provide investors with a synthesis of the academic literature on how to build evidence-based portfolios instead.

So what drives the gap between real-world portfolios based on investment narratives and scientifically sound, evidence-based portfolios? Investment narratives offered by financial advisors, internet platforms and magazines can be convincing at first and typically align with emotions and "gut feelings". They offer quick fixes to, for example, time the stock market, or provide advice on how to pick stocks. Such strategies are widespread in the world of investing, but are they delivering the expected results? We will show that resisting such investment advice is a prudent strategy for avoiding the inefficiencies that derive from narrative-based investing.

In a metaphorical sense, the situation is reminiscent of Homer's *The Odyssey*. In his epic poem, the Greek hero Odysseus embarks upon a journey home to his native Ithaca in the aftermath of the Trojan War, a voyage which takes an unexpected ten years. His return journey is arduous and marked by various challenges. One of these dangers is the seductive song of the deadly temptresses known as the Sirens. Odysseus must circumnavigate their

[1] Theories of investing and empirical research relating to stock market trading, for example, emerged in the 20th century. Some important milestones include (1) theories of investor risk preferences and decision-making under uncertainty (Savage, 1954; von Neumann and Morgenstern, 1953); (2) the development of portfolio theory (Markowitz, 1952; Roy, 1954; Tobin, 1958) (3) the development of the capital asset pricing model (CAPM), a coherent framework for answering the question how the risk of an investment should affect its expected return (Lintner, 1965; Mossin, 1966; Sharpe, 1964; Treynor, 1962) and, approximately ten years later; (4) the introduction of the combination of the CAPM with additional linear relationships between the expected return of an asset and various risk factors, in the form of arbitrage pricing theory (APT) proposed by Ross (1976).

rock and resist their piercing songs, seeking to attract and shipwreck passing mariners. In Homer's story, Odysseus resists the temptation of the Sirens by having himself tied to the mast of his ship while his rowers, their ears sealed with beeswax, sail quickly by. Resisting the fatal allure of the Sirens, as depicted in Odysseus's journey, is a prudent strategy for avoiding enticing, yet potentially detrimental distractions.

We re-frame the Homeric myth and provide a parable for those interested in an evidence-based investment approach. Like Odysseus, investors must successfully resist many temptations and master a journey without losing sight of their long-term goals, namely wealth appreciation. Their journey is made difficult by ever more tempting investment narratives. The title of our book, "The Evidence-Based Investor: From Investment Myths to Performance", describes an investor who reflects on and resists those investment strategies that are not otherwise supported by empirical evidence and instead resemble the charming, though deadly Sirens' Song.

We are aware that many financial advisors avoid taking empirical evidence seriously when assessing investment strategies. This is not very surprising. Financial advisors often act like a guild, rendering the profession insular and immune to outside criticism. Our book may doubtless invoke some anger amongst this in-group. Some might consider our book too reductionist, and we shall not be surprised. Why should we expect them to behave differently than any other group seeking to protect their profession, for example by believing in investment myths?

However, as you will see, our perspective is supported by comprehensive academic literature and the empirical evaluation of real-life investor portfolios, which shows that many popular investment strategies fail to improve performance and, in fact, lead to poor results.

To summarise in advance, investors should be aware of the following **Ten Myths of Investing**:

1. **The Market-Participation Myth**

   Most households hold solely cash and other safe assets instead of investing in capital markets. As a result, they completely miss out on the attractive opportunities that modern capital markets offer. The prevailing opinion is that only the rich and experts should invest in capital markets. However, research suggests that everyone should have at least a small portion of their assets invested in capital markets.
2. **The Investment-Concentration Myth**

   Those who invest in capital markets often hold concentrated portfolios, with capital invested in only a small number of assets. However, an under-diversified portfolio often leads to large losses, or even a total loss, and is detrimental to long-term performance. Research suggests investors should hold well-diversified portfolios for long-term capital appreciation.

3. **The Stock-Picking Myth**

   Many investors follow a stock-picking strategy, which leads to poor performance after transaction costs are taken into account. Research shows that passive strategies, which invest in whole markets rather than a selection of stocks, are likely to deliver superior performance for the vast majority of investors.

4. **The Home Bias Myth**

   Many investors are not taking advantage of the opportunity to diversify globally and are taking unnecessary risks with a concentrated portfolio of local assets. Research shows that investors should invest globally to maximise diversification and benefit from the attractive performance potential of global markets. While investing globally was costly 30 years ago, with the low-cost global investment vehicles available today, there is no excuse for not investing globally.

5. **The Active-Investing Myth**

   Even professionals who actively invest with the aim of "beating the market" are far from guaranteeing better results and yet are often following quite expensive strategies. Indeed, the literature shows that such active investor professionals, as a group, do not outperform low-cost passive strategies (net of fees). The added value of active versus passive strategies needs to be critically assessed before they are considered for investment.

6. **The Market-Timing Myth**

   It would be great to be able to buy low and sell high. However, research shows that market timing strategies do not work well enough in practice to be beneficial. They are counterproductive and tend to lead to worse performance than not trying to time the market.

7. **The Factor-Investing Myth**

   Factor investing refers to selecting stocks based on characteristics such as market capitalisation, growth, past returns, or dividends. While having strong academic roots and some historical success, factor investing sees declining returns over time, which are even smaller after considering transaction costs. Investors should ensure that they have realistic expectations of the real-world performance of factor strategies.

8. **The Performance-Persistence Myth**
   Investors believe in past performance. However, popular short-term past performance comparisons do not tell much about how an investment will perform in the future. The reason is that short-term past performance is crowded by "noise" and conveys little information concerning expected future long-term performance, which would be the relevant metric.
9. **The Volatility-Irrelevance Myth**
   It is popular to focus on returns and ignore volatility, akin to a mindset of "surely the ups and downs cancel out over time" or something to that effect. However, this is not the case. Portfolios which simply contain more risk without providing more expected return tend to perform worse in the long run. The reason for this is simple. Over time, it takes a greater increase in value to make up for a given loss. Unnecessary volatility therefore does not diversify over time, but rather constitutes a drag on long-term performance.
10. **The ESG-Investing for Performance Myth**
    Currently a big investment trend, *E*nvironment, *S*ocial and *G*overnance (ESG) investing comes with a yet unknown impact. Moreover, financial theory suggests that ESG-investing is plausibly expected to be slack in terms of long-term financial performance. Investors need to carefully compare the costs and benefits so as not to be disappointed by ESG investing.

How can the evidence-based investor escape the pernicious influence of today's Sirens of investing? How can they avoid their tempting, though potentially damaging investment narratives? As we know from Hegel's philosophy, historical developments require not only a thesis and an antithesis but also a synthesis. We therefore go beyond reviewing and debunking some of the many investment narratives that have been developed in the financial world over the past decades.

The second aim of this book is to provide a *synthesis* of scientific investment research. We suggest three easy-to-follow steps that facilitate evidence-based investing.

Step I—Invest in a global market portfolio first: Invest in a well-diversified mix of liquid financial assets, including global bonds, stocks, listed real estate, and commodities. The goal is to capture the global bond and equity premium and to make use of liquid alternative assets to further diversify risk out of the portfolio, a portfolio that can be built cost-effectively using passive mutual funds and exchange-traded funds (ETFs). While it is straightforward to passively invest in "the market" within asset classes such as equities, it is not straightforward to combine different asset classes, such as bonds and equities, in a global multi-asset market portfolio. In this book, we propose a novel approach to this unsolved problem. We show how investors can use the consensus of forward-looking institutional capital market assumptions to allocate across asset classes in a meaningful way, thereby avoiding discretionary decisions.

Step II—Consider additional investments in an "alpha" portfolio: While the global market portfolio is solid, it may not be the best boat available. Step two is to systematically look for investment opportunities that can outperform the global market portfolio on a risk-adjusted basis, and after accounting for costs. Such investments are collected in the "alpha portfolio". Because the global market portfolio sets the benchmark and is a high bar for any candidate, only a limited number of promising investments are expected to make the cut. It turns out that combining a global market portfolio with an alpha portfolio allows for an efficient mix of risky assets, one that offers the highest expected return per unit of risk. Depending on the asset class and the complexity of the strategy, the alpha portfolio may justify using more specialised and costly investment vehicles.

The alpha portfolio requires more work than the global market portfolio. Investors who prefer a simpler portfolio than an efficient portfolio may decide not to invest in the alpha portfolio and simply stick with the global market portfolio. ; More generally, there are good reasons to tailor the alpha portfolio to an individual investor's preferences. In contrast to the global market portfolio, it is not a "one size fits all" portfolio.

Step III—Manage the overall portfolio risk by investing part of the assets in a risk-free asset: Step three is all about managing risk. This involves blending the global market portfolio, the alpha portfolio, and a risk-free asset. Derivatives or complex trading strategies are NOT needed. In practice, a single "true" risk-free asset is not easily available. Investors rather rely on a portfolio of "near" risk-free assets like money-market funds, or high-quality cash deposits. This last step allows for adjustment of the total amount of risk taken without changing the expected return per unit of risk.

Each of the three sub-portfolios serves a distinct purpose and should be evaluated on its own merits. The global market portfolio aims for diversification and steers clear of investment myths, offering an attractive expected return for the risk taken. The alpha portfolio strives to enhance the global market portfolio's performance and is judged by its ability to further improve performance. The risk-free asset helps manage the overall portfolio's absolute risk, aligning it with the investor's risk tolerance. By evaluating these three sub-portfolios against their specific objectives, investors can monitor their progress towards long-term capital appreciation while avoiding the seductive, though deceptive sirens of investing.

Evidence-based portfolio management should not just be an option for portfolio management—it should be the duty of every fiduciary. While a scientific approach does not guarantee any specific performance, and past findings can sometimes be overturned, such an approach strives for the best possible outcomes based on current knowledge. By leveraging scientific insights, we can make informed decisions and manage portfolios with the highest level of responsibility and care.

Our book unfolds as follows. Chapter 2 shows that a well-diversified portfolio (i.e., one that avoids investment myths) has an impressive historical performance. These numbers give an idea of what is at stake if investors follow investment narratives and instead hold inefficient portfolios. Chapter 3 reviews the academic literature that exposes the ten investment myths, leading many investors to hold inefficient portfolios that fail to deliver a reasonable long-term performance. Chapter 4 describes the principles of an easy-to-follow evidence-based approach to investing. Falling for investment myths can be avoided by investing in a global market portfolio (Chapter 5) in conjunction with a more opportunistic alpha portfolio to further improve performance (Chapter 6) and a risk-free asset to manage the absolute risk of the portfolio (Chapter 7). Chapter 8 provides a summary of how to implement evidence-based portfolio management in practice.

References

Lintner, J. (1965). The valuation of risk assets and the selection of risky investments in stock portfolios and capital budgets. *Review of Economics and Statistics, 47*, 13–37.

Markowitz, H. (1952). Portfolio selection. *Journal of Finance, 7*, 77–91.

Mossin, J. (1966). Equilibrium in a capital asset market. *Econometrica, 34*, 768–83.

Ross, S. A. (1976). Arbitrage theory of capital asset pricing. *Journal of Economic Theory, 12*, 341–60.

Roy, A. D. (1954). Safety first and the holding of assets. *Econometrica.*

Savage, L. J. (1954). *The foundations of statistics*. Wiley.

Sharpe, W. F. (1964). Capital asset prices: A theory of market equilibrium under conditions of risk. *Journal of Finance, 19*, 425–42.

Tobin, J. (1958). Liquidity preference as behavior toward risk. *Review of Economic Studies, 25*, 65–86.

Treynor, J. L. (1962). Towards a theory of market value of risky assets. *Unpublished manuscript. Final version in Asset Pricing and Portfolio Performance* (pp. 15–22).
von Neumann, J., & Morgenstern, O. (1953). *Theory of games and economic behavior*. Princeton University Press.

2

The Performance of Simplicity

We take a look at the performance of a scientifically reasonable but very simple 50/50 buy-and-hold investment strategy that stays clear of investing myths. To this end, the historical long-term performance of a portfolio that invests 50% in global equities and 50% in government bonds is reviewed. Even though this 50/50-portfolio does not include any complex trading and investment strategy, it lead to an impressive performance: CHF 10,000 invested in 1970 would have grown to a staggering value of CHF 170,600 by the end of 2023. While there is no guarantee that such a performance will be repeated over the next 50 years, we argue that investment myths are likely to be a significant drag on long-term performance that can be avoided.

According to research, capital markets have consistently offered attractive returns over long investment horizons.[1] To illustrate the potential benefits of investing in capital markets from the viewpoint of a Swiss Francs investor, we report the performance resulting from a disciplined investment strategy and diversified portfolio held for over 50 years from January 1971 to December 2023 in Fig. 2.1.

We assume that an investor allocates 50% to a global equity portfolio and 50% to Swiss government bonds at the beginning of each year, reinvesting all dividends and interest income. This portfolio is a simplified version of a global market portfolio to get an idea of historical performance. To be conservative, we do not consider an alpha portfolio in this illustrative analysis.

[1] Academic studies on the historical performance of equities and bonds markets include (Ibbotson et al., 1985; Dimson et al., 2002, 2019; Jorda et al., 2019).

P. Böni and T. Kröncke, *The Evidence-Based Investor*,
https://doi.org/10.1007/978-3-031-88675-1_2

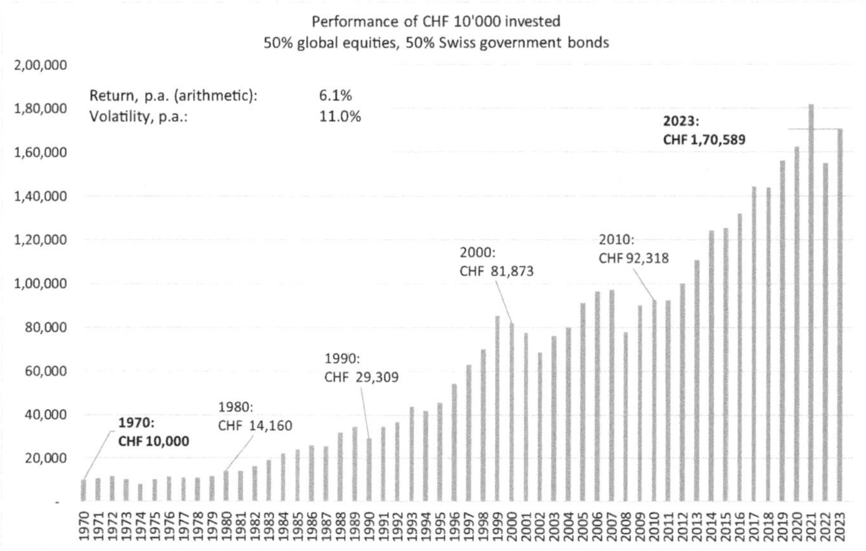

Fig. 2.1 Historical performance of a disciplined investment strategy and simple global market portfolio. This figure shows a portfolio investing 50% in global equities and 50% in Swiss government bonds using annual re-balancing. The performance of global equities is approximated by the MSCI World Index and the performance of Swiss government bonds by the Pictet Historical Swiss Bond Index, respectively. (*Source* MSCI, Pictet, own calculations)

Figure 2.1 shows that a straightforward and disciplined investment strategy, akin to keeping the ship's course steady, proves advantageous.

An investment of CHF 10,000 in 1970 would have grown to a staggering value of CHF 170,600 by the end of 2023, leading to an investment multiple of 17X over the observed period. Evidently, following such a disciplined investment approach is not always easy. The portfolio value would have increased to 'just' CHF 14,160 by the end of the 1970s. However, this value increase was achieved despite significant booms and busts in the stock markets due to the intervening oil crisis. After this turbulent period, investors had to wait until the end of the 1980s to approximately double their capital, including remarkable capital appreciations to CHF 29,309. Not a bad return! In the following run-up to the millennium, thanks in part to the dotcom boom, the capital appreciated to a value of CHF 81,873 by the end of the year 2000. Rather modest gains followed, due to the bursting of the dotcom bubble. By the end of 2010, the portfolio stood at CHF 92,318 as the global financial crisis (GFC) effectively prevented higher returns in this decade. However, the disciplined investor holding the described "simplified" global market portfolio was rewarded for being patient and calm over the next 13 years, with the value of capital nearly doubling to CHF 170,589 by 2023.

Maintaining a well-diversified portfolio and sticking to a consistent and simple strategy is essential, especially during turbulent market conditions. Contrary to this simple insight, as evidenced by a large academic literature that we summarise in Chapter 3, many investors often do not hold well-diversified portfolios. Instead, they follow inefficient strategies and achieve, on average, investment performance that is nowhere near the achievable long-term performance shown above. They often hold concentrated portfolios with excessive risk or else use investment strategies that cost more than the value they add. Investors repeatedly fall for investment myths and adopt investment strategies that may sound convincing at first, yet are likely to lead to unsatisfactory long-term investment performance.

There is no law of nature that guarantees we will experience the same long-term performance in the next 50 years as in the last 50 years. In the past, flat returns have been documented for extended periods. For example, US equities stagnated for almost two decades from 1929 to the 1940s, and Japanese equities did the same after peaking in 1989. And studies on the long-term performance of different international markets suggest that the US and the Swiss stock market are unusually successful in the past (for example, Anarkulova et al., 2022).

We will show, however, that narrative-based investors, who follow investment myths in markets that are moving downwards or sideways, add an additional and unnecessary drag to their investment performance. Investors cannot influence firms' long-term performance, which is ultimately determined by the economic success of the assets invested. Likewise, long-term economic cycles are beyond the control of an individual investor. However, investors can influence how they invest and whether or not they follow costly and largely inefficient investment myths. They can likely match a portfolio that achieves the performance comparable to that of a simple 50/50 buy-and-hold investment strategy. In contrast to the narrative-based investor, the evidence-based investor can even strive for and achieve a further improvement over the simple 50/50 investment strategy, as we will see later in this book.

References

Anarkulova, A., Cederburg, S., & O'Doherty, M. S. (2022). Stocks for the long run? Evidence from a broad sample of developed markets. *Journal of Financial Economics, 143*, 409–33.

Dimson, E., Marsh, P., & Staunton, M. (2002). *Triumph of the optimists: 101 years of global investment returns*. Princeton University Press.

Dimson, E., Marsh, P., & Staunton, M. (2019). Historical returns of the market portfolio. *The Review of Asset Pricing Studies, 10*, 521–67.

Ibbotson, R. G., Siegel, L. B., & Lovel, K. S. (1985). World wealth: Market values and returns. *Journal of Portfolio Management, 12*, 4–23.

Jorda, O., Knoll, K., Kuvshinov, D., Schularick, M., & Taylor, A. (2019). The rate of return on everything 1870–2015. *Quarterly Journal of Economics, 134*, 1225–98.

3

Ten Common Investing Myths Laid Bare

The practice of investing is reminiscent of the saga of Odysseus's sailors. The destination is known, as is the route. But the songs of the sirens are seductive and can lead to calamity on the rocks of misfortune. Just as Odysseus was seduced by the sirens' song and distracted from his ultimate goal of reaching Ithaca, so investors succumb to recurring investment myths and lose sight of their investment objective of continuous capital appreciation. We lend from extant academic research to illustrate why investment myths are seductive, yet engender sub-optimal investment decisions.

The Market-Participation Myth

The Market-Participation Myth in a nutshell: Most households hold solely cash and other safe assets instead of investing in capital markets. As a result, they completely miss out on the attractive opportunities that modern capital markets offer. The prevailing opinion is that only the rich and experts should invest in capital markets. However, research suggests that everyone should have at least a small portion of their assets invested in capital markets.

In Fig. 2.1 we have seen how participation in the financial markets with a simple investment strategy enabled investors to achieve CHF 170,600 from an initial investment of CHF 10,000 over 53 years. Such a return requires a

P. Böni and T. Kröncke, *The Evidence-Based Investor*,
https://doi.org/10.1007/978-3-031-88675-1_3

significant proportion of stocks to be held within a portfolio over a long-term period.

Despite attractive historical returns, Guiso et al. (2008) report that only about 49% of US households invest directly or indirectly in the stock market (see Table 3.1).[1] The study refers to surveys carried out around the turn of the millennium. More recent surveys, however, show no improvement over time. In 2019, equity participation in the US even fall slightly to 40%.

For European countries, stock market participation is typically even lower than in the US according to Guiso et al. (2008). For example, in Switzerland, a participation rate of 31% is reported which is on a par with many other European countries (Germany 23%, France 26%, and Italy 8%).[2] More recent data suggest an improvement for many European countries, but most of them remain well below the stock participation rate that can be observed

Table 3.1 Proportion of households investing in stocks. This table shows the stock market participation rates reported by Guiso et al. (2008). "Direct" refers to the percentage of households who directly hold shares. "Direct & Indirect" refers to the percentage of households holding shares directly or indirectly through investment funds and pension funds. US data were obtained from the Survey of Consumer Finances (SCF) and correspond to the year 1998. European data collected from the Survey of Health, Ageing and Retirement in Europe (SHARE), corresponding to the year 2003. Below the column "Updated", European SHARE data are adapted from Figure 2 in Kaustia et al. (2023) for 2013, and US SCF data are adapted from Bhutta et al. (2020) for 2019

	Guiso et al. (2008)		Kaustia et al. (2023)/Bhutta et al. (2020)
	Direct (%)	Direct and indirect (%)	Direct and indirect (%)
U.S.	19	49	40
Netherlands	17	24	20
Germany	14	23	29
Italy	4	8	10
Austria	5	9	19
Sweden	41	66	65
Spain	4	5	11
France	14	26	31
Denmark	31	37	58
Switzerland	25	31	43

[1] At the same time, the US Federal Reserve Flow of Funds statistics suggest that corporate equity, other equity, mutual fund shares and pension entitlements account for a large share, well over 50%, of financial assets. Therefore, those households that invest in the stock market also allocate a significant portion to the stock market.

[2] Earlier evidence on the low participation rate is provided by Blume and Friend (1975), Curcuru et al. (2010), Haliassos and Bertaut (1995), Mankiw and Zeldes (1991), among many others. Birchler et al. (2010) provide a more detailed discussion of the low participation rate in Switzerland.

in the US. The only countries that achieve a relative high participation rate above 50% are the Nordic countries in the sample, Sweden and Denmark in the more recent years. As can be seen, most households do not even get started with their journey!

Yet no sailor has ever reached their destination without setting off on a voyage. Studies on the historical performance of financial assets suggest that risk-free investments, like cash, hardly compensate for inflation in the long term (Ibbotson et al., 1985; Dimson et al., 2002; Doeswijk et al., 2019; Jorda et al., 2019). Also, long-term bond returns are rather meagre and are quickly eaten away during periods of unexpectedly high inflation. To realise a real increase in wealth, as illustrated in Fig. 2.1, investors must take some risk by participating in the stock market.

It might seem natural to think that sufficiently risk-averse investors should not invest in risky assets at all. However, non-participation cannot be explained by risk aversion alone. As long as stock market investments earn a positive risk premium, it is optimal to invest at least some fraction of accrued wealth in risky assets, as shown in a famous analysis by Arrow (1971) and Pratt (1964) (see Campbell, 2017 for a review of the principle of participation). For this reason, the literature has proposed many alternative explanations for non-participation in the stock market, including inertial factors, non-standard preferences, participation costs (Haliassos & Bertaut, 1995), a lack of trust in financial markets/advice (Guiso et al., 2008), intelligence (Grinblatt et al., 2011), and fear of a disastrous event (Fagereng et al., 2017).

Understandably, many investors are unfamiliar with the benefits of a relatively simple, though well-diversified portfolio. Without good guidance, they feel overwhelmed by the thousands of investments to pick from and fear falling for the sirens' chants if they travel the ocean of capital markets. As a result, they do not start their journey. However, as we will show in due course, the lack of trust in markets and financial advice, and the fear of disaster events can be overcome with an appropriate investment strategy.

The Investment-Concentration Myth

> The Investment-Concentration Myth in a nutshell: Those who invest in capital markets often hold concentrated portfolios, with capital invested in only a small number of assets. Examples of such investors include Tesla's, SpaceX's or X's Elon Musk, Microsoft's Bill Gates or the US corporate raider,

venture capitalist and later shareholder activist Carl Icahn. These figures are known to be successful investors. However, we show that holding concentrated portfolios is very risky, with under-diversified portfolios often leading to large losses, or even a total loss. Long-term investors should better hold well-diversified portfolios for long-term capital appreciation.

The equity portfolio that allocates 50% of the investment strategy shown in Fig. 2.1 is highly diversified, investing in thousands of stocks. However, concentrated portfolios that invest in very few stocks are popular in practice. For example, anecdotal evidence suggests that the "Nestlé portfolio" is quite popular among Swiss households. It comprises a single stock in the global food giant Nestlé which has an excellent track record, with an annualised geometric total return of 11.3% from January 1970 to the end of 2022. This is 1.4-fold the corresponding figure for the MSCI Swiss Country Index (a diversified investment in Swiss companies), which gained 7.8% over the same period.

More systematic evidence on underdiversification is provided in the literature. For example, Polkovnichenko (2005) investigates households in the US Survey of Consumer Finance from 1983 to 2001. Among those households which own stocks directly, the median number of stocks held was 3 in 2001 and was even lower in earlier years.[3]

But how can we tell if a portfolio is well-diversified? Portfolio theory, as pioneered by Markowitz (1952) and Tobin (1958) over 60 years ago, suggests that investors should maximise the Sharpe ratio (*SR*) of their portfolios (Sharpe, 1966):

$$SR = \frac{\mathbb{E}[R_t] - R_f}{\sigma(R_t)}.$$

As can be taken from the formula, the Sharpe ratio is based on expectations in that it applies an *ex-ante* standpoint. It refers to the expected return of a portfolio ($\mathbb{E}[R_t]$) at a given future point in time, minus the return on the risk-free asset (R_f), divided by the expected standard deviation of the portfolio ($\sigma(R_t)$). Thus, the Sharpe ratio measures the expected compensation for investing in a portfolio of risky assets (the numerator) per unit of risk taken

[3] Earlier and later studies confirm underdiversification in stock portfolios and confirm the finding across many countries, for example, see Blume and Friend (1975), Curcuru et al. (2010), Florentsen et al. (2019), Goetzmann and Kumar (2008), Kelly (1995), Kumar (2009), among many others.

(the denominator). Investors who maximise the Sharpe ratio ensure that they do not take any more risk than necessary.

Importantly, to this end, the Sharpe ratio is used to evaluate portfolios of assets and not individual assets per se. In practice, an investor could start with any portfolio and then investigate whether the addition of a particular investment increases or decreases the Sharpe ratio of the overall portfolio. The process could be repeated until the Sharpe ratio is maximized. Such an optimal portfolio is commonly referred to as an "efficient" portfolio.

While it is difficult in practice to find an "efficient" portfolio, we know that highly concentrated portfolios that invest in just a few stocks tend to be very risky and are, thus, far from the ideal of an "efficient" portfolio. Put differently, the expected return of concentrated portfolios does not sufficiently compensate for the risk taken, leading to a low Sharpe ratio. Because investors can reduce the risk of a concentrated portfolio without reducing the expected return, such portfolios are known as "underdiversified" portfolios.

Calvet et al. (2007) studied the portfolios of Swedish households with detailed information on the specific financial assets they held. They confirm that "*many Swedish households choose reasonably efficient portfolios, but a few appear to be dramatically underdiversified.*"

The return-risk trade-off for Swedish stock portfolios, taken from Calvet et al. (2007), is shown in Fig. 3.1. We see the expected return on the y-axis and the risk as measured by the standard deviation on the x-axis. Each of the dark dots in the picture shows the portfolio of a Swedish household. The red

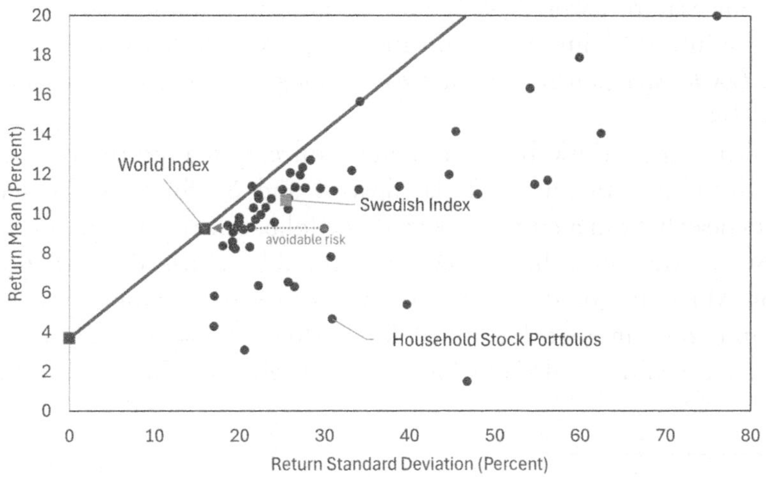

Fig. 3.1 Return and risk of Swedish households.
Return-Risk diagram for a random sample of Swedish household stock portfolios at the end of 2002. (*Source* Adapted from Calvet et al. (2007))

line is a combination of the MSCI World index portfolio and the risk-free asset (a strategy similar to the one reported in Fig. 2.1).

Because the red line starts at the risk-free rate on the y-axis, the slope of this line is equal to the Sharpe ratio of a well-diversified portfolio. Accordingly, all dark dots below this line have a Sharpe ratio that is lower and all black dots above have a Sharpe ratio that is higher than occurs with a well-diversified portfolio.

As can be seen, a considerable number of Swedish household portfolios (dark dots) are actually relatively close to the red line, although hardly any portfolios lie above the red line. Strikingly, however, a large proportion of Swedish households hold portfolios well below the red line and are clearly non-optimal. These portfolios come with an excess risk that can be attributed to underdiversification.

To give a concrete example of why this is an issue, we can pick the black dots with a standard deviation of 30% and a mean return of about 9%. By simply investing in the World Index, these investors could have achieved a portfolio with a mean return of about 9% and a standard deviation close to 20%. Several portfolios to the right of the red line also allow for a return of 9%. However, they are required to take more risk, making the realised investment outcome more volatile. As the figure shows, many household portfolios have a large potential for improvement.[4]

It appears that certain investors care more about return and to a lesser extent about risk. Indeed, holding underdiversified portfolios with only a few assets has been successful for some of the richest people on the planet. Elon Musk, for example, would likely not recommend holding a well-diversified portfolio. In a 2007 interview with Inc. magazine, Musk stated:

"*It's OK to have your eggs in one basket as long as you control what happens to that basket.*"[5]

In fact, Elon Musk holds a highly concentrated portfolio consisting primarily of investments in Tesla, SpaceX and X (formerly Twitter). He deviates heavily from a more diversified portfolio, one that invests worldwide.

However, we notice that not everyone could have held the same portfolio as Elon Musk. It would not have been possible for everyone to put everything into *the* same stocks. When Elon Musk overweights Tesla and Co. relative to a well-diversified portfolio, someone else must hold less of the same

[4] In defence of Swedish households, Calvet et al. (2007) report that many households also hold mutual funds, which are usually well-diversified. The problem of holding a concentrated portfolio, or underdiversification, is then less pronounced for the complete portfolio of financial assets for the mutual funds-owning households.

[5] Link: https://twitter.com/Inc/status/407449869646036992

companies relative to a well-diversified portfolio. Consequently, every billion of "outperformance" of Elon Musk's holdings, with respect to the world portfolio, is a billion of "underperformance" by other market participants. Unlike the highly successful Elon Musk, those unsuccessful investors holding a non-diversified portfolio are unlikely to be interviewed by a business magazine. The other side of these stellar returns is thus rarely discussed.

Yet there is another important distinction between the average investor and Elon Musk: He is an entrepreneur who utilises his voting power to control what happens to the very few eggs in his investment basket. In contrast, most investors hold relatively few shares in listed companies and therefore have very little voting power and thus little or no control over the destiny of their investments. In Elon Musk's words, they have no means of controlling what happens to their basket. As a consequence, they are well advised to diversify risk across a large number of investments.

Entrepreneurs understand the merits of portfolio diversification quite well: Look, for example, at Microsoft's Bill Gates. During his active career, his wealth was concentrated in Microsoft. But when he set up the Bill & Melinda Gates Foundation with his wife in around the year 2000, he transferred a significant portion of his wealth to the foundation. The foundation adopted a well-diversified investment approach to reduce risk and fund its activities over the long run. While the exact positions of the foundation's portfolio are not known, one can see from the financial statement that the trust is diversified across industries and asset classes.[6] Indeed, the foundation's asset manager's website states that it "...applies a fundamental, long-term investment approach across asset classes and geographies".[7]

Carl Icahn is another example we want to mention: He is a prominent figure in American finance, corporate raider and venture capitalist, later in his career a shareholder activist. A billionaire investor, Icahn initially adopted a contrarian investment strategy, targeting undervalued or overlooked stocks with the intent to restructure or break up underlying businesses and divest their assets. His high-profile transactions—such as his involvement in RJR Nabisco in the late 1990s, Time Warner in 2006, and Netflix Inc. in 2012—have bolstered his reputation as a successful investor. In each of these cases, Icahn's strategy adhered to a contrarian activist model, characterized by a concentrated investment approach. However, more recently the inherent risks of this concentrated strategy have negatively affected Icahn's financial position. Over the past years, his firm, Icahn Enterprises, has faced significant challenges. For example, its largest holding, CVR Energy, has experienced

[6] https://www.gatesfoundation.org/, retrieved on November 4, 2024.

[7] https://cascadeassetmanagement.com/, retrieved on November 4, 2024.

operational and market-related difficulties. Reflecting the risk associated with a high-concentration investment philosophy, Icahn Enterprises' stock price declined sharply, from over $50 at the end of 2022 to approximately $10 by the start of the fourth quarter of 2024. The shareholder's five-year return of an investment in Icahn Enterprises is negative by more than 80%.[8] This development underscores the potential vulnerabilities even seasoned investors like Icahn face when managing highly concentrated portfolios.[9]

Kumar (2009) gets to the heart of the matter. A heavily underdiversified portfolio is like a lottery ticket that offers, with some probability, great riches. It is reasonable that some investors participate in the stock market to play what might be called the "stock market lottery", rather than focusing on building efficient portfolios. But what are the odds that a single stock portfolio makes one rich, begging the question as to whether the "stock market lottery" is an attractive risk?

Empirical evidence however suggests that this is not the case. Bessembinder (2018) finds that the lifetime performance of single stock portfolios is heavily skewed, with the chances of underperforming the overall market being much higher than outperforming it.[10] He studied the distribution of single stock returns in the US from 1926 to 2016. Historically, only 30.8% of stocks have a lifetime buy-and-hold return that exceeds the US market portfolio, while only 40.2% of stocks have outperformed the risk-free rate. More importantly, the most frequently observed lifetime buy-and-hold return on a single stock portfolio is a loss of between 95% and 100%. In terms of dollar wealth created, the numbers are even more skewed. The stock market premium over the risk-free rate is driven by very few stocks represented in the index, specifically by only the top 4% of all firms represented in the index. The remaining 96% of firms only matched the performance of the risk-free rate. It follows that one has to cherry-pick only those very few exceptional stocks. In other words, the probability of losing almost everything with a single-stock or badly diversified portfolio is considerable. Despite this, many investors remain underdiversified, following an investment strategy more akin to that of a lottery. They copy the 'Elon Musks' of the world, but forget that they have little or no control over the performance of their investments.

Thus, many investors fall for the investment concentration myth in that they do not judge their portfolio by the return relative to the risk offered.

---

8 As retrieved from Yahoo Finance on November 21, 2025. Ticker:IEP.

9 See Financial Times article "Key Icahn holding sputters in latest blow to this corporate empire", dated October 31, 2024.

10 Bessembinder and Wei (2023) confirm the findings for the US stockmarket for international markets, including Switzerland.

Perhaps they do not know any better, or find that holding a well-diversified portfolio is boring. While a portfolio that essentially covers the entire market is unsuited to interesting small talk at a party or when meeting friends on the golf course, the odds of it beating a concentrated portfolio are very high. So why not avoid underdiversification by holding a well-diversified long-term market portfolio, whilst pursuing a more speculative strategy in a smaller, separate portfolio?

Shefrin and Statman (2000) suggests that investors could split their investments into two portfolios; one a well-diversified portfolio designed to achieve long-term capital appreciation, and the other a portfolio designed to play the lottery (i.e., a "speculative portfolio"). This strategy of employing separate accounts for separate objectives allows investors to satisfy their speculative appetite without exposing their main portfolio to inappropriate levels of risk.

The Stock-Picking Myth

The Stock-Picking Myth in a nutshell: Stock-picking is likely to lead to poor performance after transaction costs are taken into account. The literature suggests that financial analysts' forecasts for stocks and credit rating insights from rating agencies are not helpful for selecting investments. Instead, it shows that passive strategies, which invest in whole markets rather than a selection of stocks, are likely to deliver superior performance for the vast majority of investors.

The equity part of the investment strategy shown in Fig. 2.1 is invested across the entire market. This means that an investor simply buys all available stocks in proportion to their market capitalisation or, more conveniently, one invests in an index such as the MSCI World Index (as assumed in Fig. 2.1). Investors who wish to consider only stocks from a specific single country as the investment universe may use the S&P 500 for the US equity market, for example, or the SPI for the Swiss equity market. This way of buying the market is straightforward and has become known as passive investing.[11]

[11] The weights of a market portfolio, which holds securities in proportion to market capitalisation, change in line with relative performance and no trading is required. It is therefore deemed a "passive" investment strategy. Sometimes practitioners and academics use an equally weighted portfolio as a proxy for the market. However, such a portfolio has fixed weights and is, in that sense, active. Over time, you need to rebalance away from stocks that are rising in value and towards stocks that are falling in value to keep the weights equal.

Stock picking or, more generally, security picking, refers to strategies in which investors actively trade in the market with the goal of outperforming the market. In contrast to a "passive" market portfolio, stock picking is considered an "active" investment strategy.

The empirical evidence for successful stock picking is, however, rather depressing. As illustrated above, picking certain stocks and holding them long-term comes with bad odds (Bessembinder, 2018). The majority of stocks come with a meagre long-term performance, as only a few stocks contribute to the market's overall success.

Perhaps frequent trading improves the chances of achieving a more favourable performance. We can say in advance, however, that this appears not to be the case. Frequent trading requires the investor not only to outperform the market, but also to earn back the costs of trading, and these costs weigh heavily. In their seminal study, Barber and Odean (2000) found that those households which actively traded generate a gross return that is about the same as investors who trade relatively little. When excluding transaction costs, these investors earn about the same amount of money. In other words, for the heavy traders, every "good" trade tends to be offset by a "bad" trade. However, bear in mind that trading is associated with costs. After considering transaction costs, investors who trade a lot clearly underperform, on average.

The main finding of Barber and Odean (2000) is presented in Fig. 3.2. The grey bars show gross returns, the black bars show net returns, i.e. returns after considering transaction costs, and the red bars show the difference between the two (in red). A first and important observation is that there is little difference in gross performance between high-turnover and low-turnover investors (20.2%, column 5, vs. 19.3%, column 1). In sharp contrast to this observation, low-turnover investors (column 1) have much higher net returns than high-turnover investors (column 5). Net returns decrease monotonically as a function of turnover and the difference in the annual return between a low-turnover investor (column 1) to a high-turnover investor (column 5) amounts to a significant 7.5%. Barber and Odean (2000) also show in their study that passive retail investors investing in the S&P 500 Index Fund are better off, in terms of net returns, than the average individual investor, and much better off than the investor implementing a high turnover strategy.

The Barber-Odean finding for retail investors has been confirmed by numerous studies, and these are summarised in literature surveys such as Campbell (2006) or, more recently, in Gomes et al. (2021). It appears prudent to say that non-professional investors, as a group, are not generally successful in stock picking. We can thus claim that empirical evidence

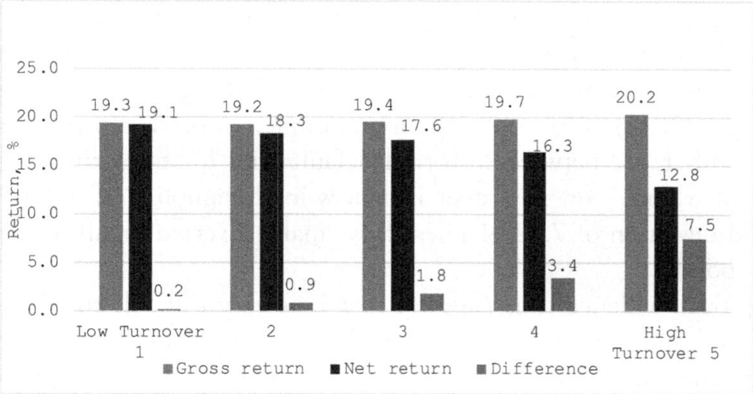

Fig. 3.2 Portfolio turnover and performance.
This figure shows the average return of investor portfolios sorted by portfolio turnover. Annualized gross returns (grey bar) and net returns (black bar) for the low-turnover and high-turnover investor are in columns one and five respectively. The red bar shows the difference between gross and net returns. (*Source* Adapted from Barber and Odean (2000), available at SSRN http://dx.doi.org/10.2139/ssrn.219228)

does not support the assumption that investors can easily beat the market by picking stocks. Indeed, the opposite is the case.

So perhaps non-professional investors should put more weight on reading financial analyst reports and follow analysts' investment advice more closely. Unfortunately, such a "quick-fix" does not exist: It is well-documented that financial analysts exhibit biases in their forecasts (see Lim, 2002 or, more recently, Pursiainen, 2022 for more information on observed analyst biases). In fact, to err is human, and analysts often provide earnings predictions that are not very helpful in picking stocks. Cao et al. (2024) document that the likelihood of financial analysts making extreme errors is quite large. In their empirical study, they benchmark the forecast error to the 90th percentile of prediction errors from all analysts in the same firm over the same year. They discovered that the likelihood analysts make extreme errors (surpassing the 90th percentile threshold) is above 9%. The likelihood of generating a prediction error larger than the 75th percentile threshold is at an even higher 16.8%. As established by Barber et al. (2001), trading stocks based on analysts' consensus recommendations requires high trading levels which entail substantial transaction costs. In line with this contention, the latter strategy leads to net returns over the market portfolio that are not reliably greater than zero.

Selecting investment bonds, for want of an additional security-selection example, is often based on credit ratings. Such ratings tend to substantially affect bond prices. However, the credit rating industry provides inflated ratings during booms when investors are more trusting (Bolton et al., 2012). Moreover, credit ratings are updated with significant time delays, resulting in stark credit rating divergence amongst rating agencies (Cornaggia & Cornaggia, 2013). Akins (2018), for example, shows a remarkable mean implied difference between historical default rates for the ratings issued by S&P and Moody's on new debt issuances in the amount of 4.2%, with a standard deviation of 7.32%! These flaws make it very difficult for investors to pick bonds.

Empirical evidence thus suggests that it is very difficult to select either stocks or bonds or to improve the odds by simply following a financial advisor's investment recommendations or ratings. Even if we just try hard enough to select the right stocks or bonds, this evidence suggests that it is very difficult to outperform the market by security selection. Millions of investors compete on the capital markets with other investors, and competition between investors leads to good deals evaporating due to a functioning market.[12] While competition cannot fully drive out asset mispricing, even in functioning markets (Grossman & Stiglitz, 1980), finding the right stock-picking opportunities is notoriously difficult and costly.

The Active-Investing Myth

> The Active-Investing Myth in a nutshell: Even professionals who actively invest with the aim of "beating the market" are far from guaranteeing better results and yet are often following quite expensive strategies. Indeed, the literature shows that such active investor professionals, as a group, do not outperform low-cost passive strategies (net of fees). We elaborate on the decline in direct holdings of equities over the past decade and the rise of delegated asset management. We suggest that the added value of active versus passive strategies needs to be critically assessed, and, importantly, that exchange-traded funds (ETFs) should be considered in order to profit from low-cost investing, liquidity and passive index tracking.

As pointed out by Sharpe (1991), the "arithmetic of active management" suggests that the sum of all active investment strategies must also be equivalent to the market portfolio. If one "active" investor wants to hold relatively more Coca-Cola shares than the market, it follows that another

[12] The emphasis is on "good deals", i.e. an outperformance that is easy to realise.

"active" investor must hold relatively fewer. Accordingly, the sum of active investment strategies cannot outperform the market before trading and management costs. In fact, they must underperform the market after trading and management costs.

However, not all active investors have to be the same. For example, the results by Barber and Odean (2000) suggest that households are unsuccessful when they follow active trading strategies. Therefore, there may be plenty of opportunities for active professional investors to profit from the mistakes of active non-professional investors. Furthermore, Pedersen (2018) argues that even real-life market portfolios are not perfectly passive and in fact require at least some trading. For example, due to share issues, share buybacks and index rebalancing—another opportunity for professionals opens up to be on the "right" side of active management and to "beat the market". Unfortunately, the academic literature finds that this is actually not so easy.

French (2008), in his presidential address to the American Finance Association, compared the fees, expenses, and trading costs society pays to invest with professional fund managers in the US stock market with an estimate of what would be paid if everyone invested passively. Averaging for the period from 1980-2006, he found that investors spent 0.67% of the aggregate value of the market each year searching for superior returns. This means that active professional investors must outperform active non-professional investors sufficiently well to win back the costs they charge.

Evidence from mutual funds managers suggests that professionals, as a group, outperform the market somewhat before fees but underperform after fees (e.g., Carhart, 1997; Kosowski et al., 2006; Harvey & Liu, 2022). Thus, there is indeed evidence that professionals, as a group, profit from the investment mistakes of the layman. However, the amount earned is not enough to offset what they charge.

However, not all active professional investors have to be the same. While the mutual fund managers, as a group, do not outperform the market after fees, there may be some mutual fund managers who do. However, there is not much scientific evidence that many fund managers are indeed so highly "skilled". Most outperformance within the group of mutual fund managers can be attributed to "luck". Empirical findings vary somewhat, particularly due to the methodology applied, but basically range from the conclusion that there is "almost no skill" involved (Carhart, 1997; Fama & French, 2010) to a "relatively modest portion of skill" among fund managers (Kosowski et al., 2006; Harvey & Liu, 2022). Cremers et al. (2019) provide a comprehensive review of the relevant literature. They point out that the empirical evidence on skill for professional fund managers is more positive in smaller markets and when looking at more specific subgroups of fund managers, environs in which the existence of skill is more plausible.

What about institutional investors, such as banks, insurance companies, pension funds, and other large financial corporations? We entrust much of our wealth to these institutions. They manage, for example, our pension schemes. Do they possess skills to outperform the market? Lewellen (2011) studies the performance of such institutional investors in the US, exploiting SEC filings on their asset holdings. He does not find evidence in favour of outperforming the market when looking at a broader definition of professional investors, at least one that goes beyond mutual funds.

In a recent study, Gerakos et al. (2021) look at an even more specialised subset of institutional investors who invest on behalf of pension funds, endowments, and other large clients. The database comes from an asset management consultant advising large institutional investors. The study of the performance of this highly competitive and professional segment of asset management shows that they outperform the market, after costs, by a modest 31 basis points, or 0.31%, per annum. However, this outperformance is not due to stock-picking skills and can be explained by factor investing strategies which, as we see later, have tended to decline in terms of performance over recent years.

It is important to notice, that these institutional investors have an estimated total cost of approximately 80 basis points or 0.8% per year (Gerakos et al., 2021). This amount includes administration and all transaction costs and is less than what is often charged to non-institutional or private investors.

Some active mutual funds charge management fees of between 1% and 2%. In addition, advisor fees, trading commissions, and trading costs (such as the bid-ask spread) come on top of that—resulting in even higher overall costs.[13] Thus, active mutual funds would have to perform way better than the institutional investors in the study of Gerakos et al. (2021) to be able to deliver outperformance net of costs. Investors should thus not be indifferent

[13] To cite an example, holding mutual funds comes with costs. Imagine, for instance, that your financial advisor buys mutual funds into your portfolio. Empirical studies show that management expenses for mutual funds, which are charged in proportion to the investment value, are substantial. Hitzemann et al. (2022) find average expenses for active US mutual funds in the amount of 1.4%, while Linnainmaa et al. (2021) find average mutual fund fees for active Canadian mutual funds in the amount of 2.4%. So for that portion of your portfolio allocated to mutual funds, you will likely bear additional expenses independent of the financial advisor's fees and trading commission, i.e. you will bear layered fees for the same set of assets. On top of mutual fund costs, the investor bears the trading commissions associated with buying and selling the assets. Moreover, there will be the financial advisor's fee. In a simple calculation, if the investor pays a financial advisor fee of 50 basis points and trades a mutual fund for another 50 basis points (including the acquisition and disposal of the fund) every five years, then the total cost of holding this fund could be as high as 2% p.a. (1.4% + 0.5% + [0.20*0.5%]).

between higher-cost and lower-cost managers, unless there is evidence that the first are producing significant (risk-adjusted) outperformance.

But also holding and trading stocks and options, which is common to many investors, may be expensive: The direct costs[14] consist of the financial advisor's fee (let's assume 50 basis points), bid-ask spreads when stocks are traded, and trading commissions. Ardia et al. (2024) show that the average spread for trading stocks amounts to an approximate 70 basis points. Each stock trade will thus likely cost the so-called effective half-spread in the approximate amount of 35 basis points. For options, the spread is much higher. Muravyev and Pearson (2020) find that the effective half-spread paid by investors that buy or sell options accounts for an average of 2.5% of the option price. If we add trading commissions in the amount of 25 basis points and the financial advisor's fee in the amount of 50 basis points, holding stocks that are regularly traded (once a year) comes at an approximate cost of 1.5% (0.7% + 0.25% + 0.5%). Investors that actively trade options will have costs that are larger by some 4.3% (+5% −0.7%). Additional costs may occur from investing in hedge funds, structured products or the exchange rate margin of banks, the difference between the wholesale exchange rate (or the interbank rate) and the rate offered to the portfolio owner. Adding all these costs up may lead to high costs of holding an active portfolio of securities.

According to French (2008), holding hedge funds, to make another impactful point, costs investors an annual combined fee (management fee and performance fee) in the amount of 3.69% annually for the period 2000 through 2007. So the hedge fund industry must generate risk-adjusted returns that exceed this cost for the investor to break even. This is, as we know by now, very difficult.

Over recent decades, we have seen a rise in delegated asset management. As shown in Fig. 3.3, we observe a relative decline in household direct holdings, such as equities. On the other hand, as represented by the rise in delegated management in Fig. 3.3, passive investment strategies have become increasingly popular.

The growth of delegated portfolio management, particularly in relation to increasing investor demand for passive investments, is largely driven by their cost-efficiency and high liquidity. Easley et al. (2021) report that passive ETFs entail management fees of around 5–30 basis points. The cost advantages of implementing passive investing can thus be considerable.

---

[14] We only refer to likely direct out-of-pockets costs in this example. We do not refer to opportunity costs arising from making (bad) investment decisions that may lead to a portfolio's underperformance relative to the market return here.

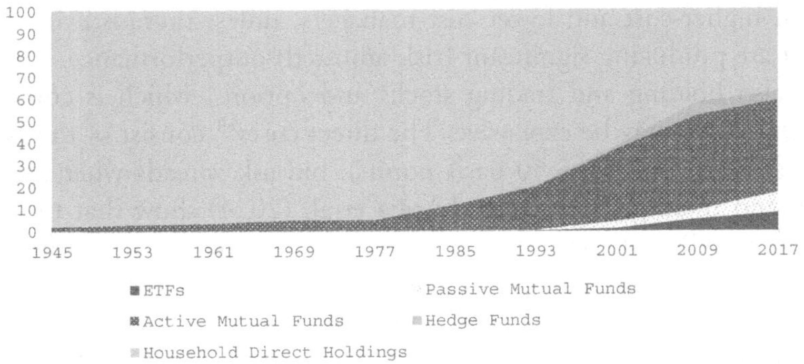

Fig. 3.3 The decline in direct holdings (Equities) and the rise of delegated management.
This figure shows the decline in household direct holdings and the rise of delegated management, including active mutual funds and hedge funds, passive mutual funds and exchange-traded funds (ETFs). The data come from the Federal Reserve's Flow of Funds Report, except the hedge fund data, which derive from HFR, and the breakdown of mutual fund holdings into active versus passive, courtesy of Morningstar. *Source* Adapted from Gârleanu and Pedersen (2022), available at SSRN http://dx.doi.org/10.2139/ssrn.3253537

However, management fees may well be justified as two simple criteria must be met to justify them. First, the strategy must be truly active, otherwise a high fee cannot be justified. This is not self-evident. Cremers and Petajisto (2009) find that a surprisingly large share of US mutual funds are actually close to being passive funds in terms of their portfolio composition. Second, when investing a part of the portfolio in an active rather than passive strategy, the return must increase by more than the additional fee that is now charged. Otherwise, an investor would be still better off by not investing in the active strategy. For example, if a fund enables an elevated risk-adjusted return of 3.0%, an all-in fee of 1.5% means that the investment still allows an increase in performance, net of fees.

The "active investing myth", namely that professional or smart investors can easily beat the market, should be challenged. Active strategies must overcome a high hurdle before adding such proponents to a portfolio. There has to be evidence of a clear value added after all fees are taken into account.

The flip side is that passive strategies can plausibly make up the majority, or even the entire portfolio if an investor is unable to find such evidence. Ten to twenty years ago, building a globally diversified passive portfolio in a cost-efficient way would have been difficult. However, the advent of ETFs, in particular, has changed this. We agree with Ben-David et al. (2017)[15] who write (p. 185):

> *ETFs are perhaps the greatest game-changer in the asset management industry in the first decades of the twenty-first century. These investment vehicles offer a combination of features that have not been available to investors before: low-cost transactions, intraday liquidity, and passive index tracking.*

The Home-Bias Myth

> The Home-Bias Myth in a nutshell: Many investors are not taking advantage of the opportunity to diversify globally. They take unnecessary risks with a concentrated portfolio of local assets. We introduce research that shows that investors should invest globally to maximize diversification and benefit from the attractive performance potential of global markets.

Many investors heavily prioritise domestic over international assets (French & Poterba, 1991; Lewis, 1999; Kalok Chan & Ng, 2005; Choi et al., 2017). They buy assets they believe they know better, thereby falling prey to the home-bias myth. In fact, they are missing out on the opportunity for international diversification. Such benefits were documented more than 50 years ago (Grubel, 1968; Levy & Sarnat, 1970). Look, for example, at the home bias of Swiss pension funds. Of the 50 largest Swiss pension funds, 43 make their share of Swiss companies in their respective equity portfolios publicly available. Their home bias is revealed in Fig. 3.4.

The share of Swiss companies in the MSCI World Index, a value-weighted global equity market portfolio, is around 2.5%. An internationally diversified equity portfolio should, therefore, not hold an allocation in Swiss companies that exceeds this number substantially. In reality, among large Swiss pension funds, eight allocate between 10% and 19.9% to Swiss companies. These are the ones with the lowest home bias as 33 pension funds allocate between 20% and 49.9% to local equity markets. Two pension funds allocate over 50% to Swiss equities! These pension funds could achieve the same expected return while taking less risk by simply investing more globally.

[15] Ben-David et al. (2017) provide an interesting description of the evolution of the ETF market over the past decades. The interested reader may also find information related to the mechanisms of ETFs, the rise of passive investing, and ETFs' impact on asset prices in their paper.

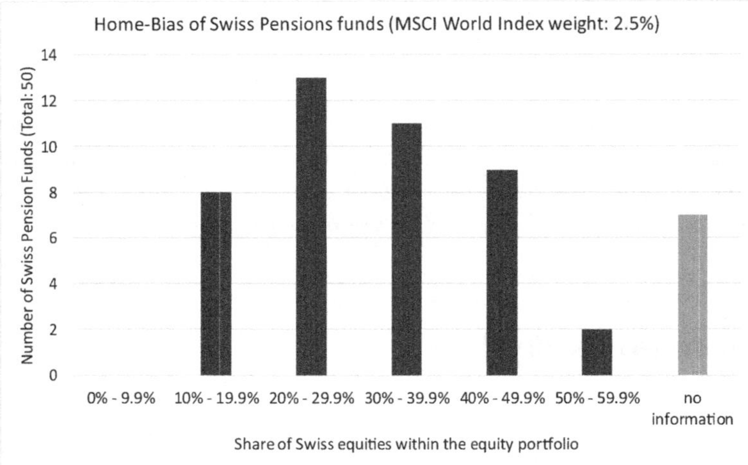

Fig. 3.4 Home bias of Swiss pension funds.
This figure shows the share of Swiss companies in the equity portfolio among the 50 largest Swiss pension funds. The figure reports the data from 43 Swiss pension funds which publish such information. *Source* Own calculations

Popular explanations for the home bias include a lack of access to international markets, high transaction costs, information advantages over local companies, and hedging motives. In times when cost-efficient ETFs can easily be selected and held, and with the global flow of information made possible by modern communication technology, the first two explanations appear unconvincing to us. Another idea is that Swiss stocks help to reduce risks specific to Swiss investors. For example, if labour income decreases in Switzerland and, concurrently, Swiss stocks go up, they would serve to hedge Swiss labour income (Mayers, 1973). Swiss stocks then become more attractive to Swiss investors than, for example, a Japanese investor. However, such a channel is not plausible. It is more likely that if Swiss labour income suffers, then Swiss equities will also suffer, and there are not many hedging benefits to be hoped for. If anything, foreign equities should be less correlated with Swiss labour income and have better hedging characteristics. According to this logic, it is more plausible for Swiss investors to underweight Swiss companies.

The Swiss equity market is far from representative in terms of the global equity market portfolio in terms of diversification across industries as it is heavily weighted towards the healthcare and consumer goods sectors. So, apart from the risk of missing the "right" individual companies (Bessembinder, 2018), the home-biased investor even bears the risk of missing the "right" industries.

Investors, particularly those from smaller countries, should avoid a home bias. The logic of competitive markets suggests that foreign stocks are equally fair priced as domestic stocks–independent of where the investor is domiciled. Investing more broadly leads to more diversification and also allows investors to benefit from industries or the success of companies that do not happen to trade in their home country.

The Market-Timing Myth

The Market-Timing Myth in a nutshell: We critically assess the traditional "buy low, sell high" investment advice. We delve into a range of commonly referenced stock price predictors, including dividend yield, term spread, implied volatility, trend indicators, corporate activity, and economic activity. By reviewing research that tests these predictors, we find that market timing strategies based on these indicators often result in poorer performance compared to a consistent, long-term investment approach that avoids market timing. This analysis highlights the limitations and potential pitfalls of attempting to predict market movements.

So what about market timing? Can investors successfully time markets, rather than focusing purely on the composition of a portfolio? In the 1960s and 1970s, this question would have been answered by a straight "no, stock markets follow a random walk". The conventional wisdom, at this time, was that the stock market, as a whole, more or less moved randomly (Cootner, 1964; Samuelson, 1965; Fama, 1970). The rationale is that competition among investors ensures that share prices immediately reflect all available information (the so-called *Efficient Market Hypothesis*). As new information reaches the market randomly, so stock price changes were also considered to be purely random. From a random walk perspective, market timing can thus only outperform a buy-and-hold strategy due to luck. After accounting for transaction costs, market timing was thus expected to underperform, in the long run.

The random walk view has since been abandoned by the academic literature. In the 1980s, particularly as a result of the seminal work of Shiller (1981) and the literature that followed. Shiller (1981) presented the following interesting thought experiment: He used a historical dataset to calculate the fair price of a stock market index at each point in time, assuming that investors would be able to (i) forecast future dividends perfectly, and (ii) discount these dividends with a constant expected return. He then compared the evolution of the perfect foresight stock price, which can be interpreted as a fundamental value, with the actual stock price observed. An updated version of the Shiller thought experiment is shown in Fig. 3.5 (Shiller, 2014). Shiller found that the actual stock prices oscillates around its fundamental value. Accordingly, investors should be able to predict stock returns, or at least to some degree. Periods in which the price is above the fundamental value should be followed by periods with a stock price closer to, or below the fundamental value.

Indeed, Shilller's evidence was quickly supplemented by studies showing that, not only by examining dividends relative to the stock price, but also additional macroeconomic factors, such as interest rates, help to predict actual stock returns (Campbell & Shiller, 1988a, 1988b; Fama & French, 1988, 1989). In fact, Shiller's notion of excess volatility and the return predictability phenomenon are in fact two sides of the same coin. If there is a predictable component in stock prices, one would expect to find "excess volatility" (Campbell & Shiller, 1988a; Cochrane, 1991). Until today, the search for

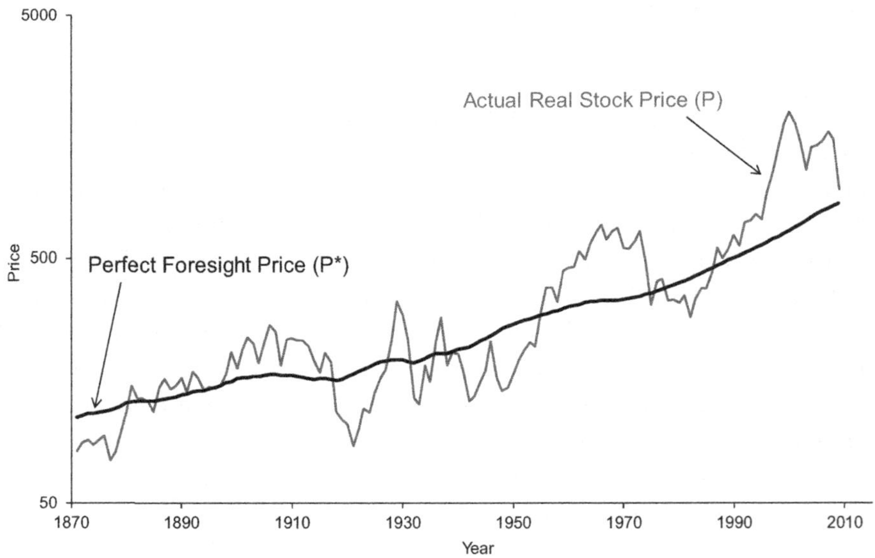

Fig. 3.5 Observed price of the market portfolio and its perfect foresight price. This figure shows the difference between the perfect foresight price and the realized price. The perfect foresight price is equal to the future realised dividends discounted by a constant rate of return. The realised price is much more volatile than the "fundamental value" implied by dividends. (*Source* Adapted from Shiller (2014), available at SSRN http://dx.doi.org/10.2139/ssrn.2391284)

return predictors remains an active topic of research within the literature. A selection of popular stock price predictors includes:

- the dividend yield and related fundamental ratios (e.g., Campbell & Shiller, 1988a, 1988b; Fama & French, 1988);
- the term-spread and other bond yields and spreads (e.g., Keim & Stambaugh, 1986; Campbell, 1987; Fama & French, 1989);
- implied volatility and related variables (e.g., Bollerslev et al., 2009; Bakshi et al., 2011; Martin, 2017);
- trend signals (e.g., Moskowitz et al., 2012; Li & Yu, 2012; Neely et al., 2014);
- corporate activity (e.g., Baker & Wurgler, 2000; Hirshleifer et al., 2009);
- and economic activity (e.g., Cochrane, 1991; Lettau & Ludvigson, 2001; Cooper & Priestley, 2009; Atanasov et al., 2020).

Shiller's model and the empirical findings listed above have led to a complete rethink in finance. It appeared to be quite possible to predict stock returns over time and a literature emerged proposing rational and behavioural explanations for observed stock returns. Robert Shiller and Eugene Fama, together with Lars Peter Hansen, were awarded the Sveriges Riksbank Prize for Economic Sciences in Memory of Alfred Nobel in 2013 "for their empirical analysis of asset prices".[16]

But does market timing really work in practice? Unfortunately, we find little support for market timing as an investment strategy when considering the following facts:

First, the empirical evidence summarised above suggests that stock prices remain "expensive" for several years, sometimes for as long as a decade. Stock prices thus appear to be predictable for a (very) long horizon only, while market timing is typically done in the hope of profiting from price swings in the short- to medium-term. The empirical evidence thus supports a "dynamic asset allocation" only at a low frequency, but does not support fast-moving timing strategies that aim to exploit weekly or monthly market price variations. With shorter horizons (e.g., daily or hourly), so-called market microstructure effects give rise to a predictable component in stock returns, especially for less liquid assets (e.g., Roll, 1984). For example, when markets are thin, it is possible that some investors willingly overpay for fast access to certain stocks, which allows those who provide liquidity to earn some extra returns. However, such market microstructure effects are hard to exploit

[16] https://www.nobelprize.org/prizes/economic-sciences/2013/press-release/.

in practice for most investors. The required trading strategies come with trading costs that typically outweigh the gains from short-term trading. Only specialised investors who can trade "more cheaply than the average Joe" are likely to be able to successfully trade on such signals (commonly known as high-frequency traders).

Second, it is unclear precisely what economic mechanisms cause cyclical stock market valuations. Shiller (2000) likes to use the notion of mispricing to explain return predictability. He believes that investors become (too) excited about asset markets and this leads to exuberance, in that they are prepared to pay prices that are, relative to their fundamental value, too high. This leads to an irrational boom in asset prices, which ultimately collapse at some future point in time. The result of such investor exuberance is a cyclical pattern in asset price valuations that "smart" investors seek to exploit. However, understanding this cyclical pattern induced by investor exuberance is very difficult. On the other hand, predictability could also be caused by a time variation in expected returns, as emphasised by Fama and French (1988). In "good times", investors might be willing to take on more risk. All else being equal, they would be prepared to accept a lower required return, which in turn pushes asset prices up. In "bad times", investors might want to de-risk. All else being equal, they would increase the required return, pushing asset prices down. However, in reality, it is utterly difficult to detect mispricing or the temporal variation in expected returns. In both cases, an investor would have to think and act like a contrarian (i.e., to sell when buying is popular and vice versa). However, being a contrarian is easier said than done.

Third, documenting predictability in an academic study based on a large sample and a long historical observation period on the one side, and investing based on such models in real time on the other, is an entirely different pair of shoes. While Campbell & Shiller (1988a) and Fama & French (1988) and others estimate econometric models to predict returns within a given sample, investors must first estimate a model and then invest "out-of-sample". This leads to the discovery of another worm in the apple. The work of Goyal and Welch (2008) shows that in-sample predictors (including the dividend yield) fail to predict asset prices in an out-of-sample exercise. In other words, it is considerably more difficult to predict asset prices in real time than in an academic study using historical data. Recently, Goyal et al. (2021) updated their analysis with newly proposed predictors. They find that still, no predictor works consistently out-of-sample. We may thus claim that researchers have still not found those factors which reliably predict stock returns out-of-sample.

But what generates the discrepancy between the in-sample and out-of-sample results? Cochrane (2008) shows that poor out-of-sample predictability is driven by the fact that the predictable component of stock returns is only relatively small. Yet, stock returns are volatile and, accordingly, the signal-to-noise ratio is bad and hard to detect in small samples. In practice, things get even worse when compared to the hypothetical world for various reasons. For example, the dividend yield can be mismeasured (e.g., Boudoukh et al., 2007; Koijen & Nieuwerburgh, 2011; Jank, 2015), or the true relationship between future returns and the predictor might be subject to structural breaks (Lettau & Nieuwerburgh, 2008).

But it gets even worse. Among the many predictors proposed in the literature, at least some are likely to be subject to data mining. This means that the documented relationship is spurious and the result of repeated testing lies in contradiction to a true relationship. An amusing study by Novy-Marx (2014) shows that "the party of the US president, the weather in Manhattan, global warming, the El Niño phenomenon, sunspots, and the conjunctions of the planets all have significant power predicting the performance of popular anomalies". While these variables are not economically relevant predictors, Novy-Marx (2014) data mined them to illustrate the severity of the problem. Be honest! Would you invest in a model that uses these predictors? We are sure that you would rather not!

Should investors then engage in market timing given these challenges? The answer requires a nuanced perspective. First, short-horizon predictability is not empirically documented beyond difficult-to-exploit market microstructure effects. However, profiting from such effects requires the ability to trade at very low cost. The latter is a precondition to exploit such market microstructure effects. In the absence of very low transaction costs, short-horizon trades are unprofitable for most investors. Second, there is no consistent empirical evidence which suggests that it is possible to avoid downturns due to an unexpected economic crisis. The COVID-19 pandemic crisis is such an example. Such downturns may come with serious costs.[17] Third, the work of Shiller, Fama, and others suggests that contrarian strategies, where investors overweight cheap assets and underweight expensive assets, are beneficial from a performance perspective in the long run. However, it requires patience and the capacity to overcome practical difficulties. Finally, not everyone can be a contrarian, by definition. Given available empirical

[17] It is possible to avoid downturns by using, for example, the help of derivatives with insurance-like payoffs. Such insurance strategies are usually relatively expensive and do not come without costs for investors (e.g., Welch, 2016).

research and what we have discussed, there is no good reason to place great hopes upon market timing strategies.

The Factor-Investing Myth

> The Factor-Investing Myth in a nutshell: Do certain firm characteristics predict stock returns and does using those factors allow investors to select assets for performing investment strategies? We present empirical evidence that challenges this view. Factor performance drops significantly after their discovery, and transaction costs are taken into account. Moreover, the economic mechanism behind many factors remains a mystery.

While the scientific literature provides little support for discretionary stock picking, as previously discussed, there is a large literature supporting the idea that certain specific firm characteristics help to select stocks that allow for investment outperformance. Factor investing simply means tilting toward a diversified group of stocks that share a certain common characteristic, and this common characteristic is considered to predict returns. The list of such factor strategies is long.[18] Among the best-known stock characteristics that predict stock returns are:

- Market capitalisation (Banz, 1981), known as the size factor;
- Book-to-market ratio (Rosenberg et al., 1985), known as the value factor;
- Past performance (Jegadeesh & Titman, 1993), known as the momentum factor;
- Investment growth (Cooper et al., 2008), known as the investment factor;
- Profitability (Novy-Marx, 2013), known as the profitability factor, or quality factor;
- Beta (Frazzini & Pedersen, 2014), known as the betting against beta, or defensive factor.

The profitability of factor-investing strategies is often illustrated in research in the form of portfolios that buy stocks which are predicted to perform well while selling stocks that are predicted to perform badly. For example, the seminal work by Fama and French (1992; 1993; 1996) showed that

[18] See, for example, the "list of factors" compiled by Hou et al. (2015), or Chen and Zimmermann (2022).

the Sharpe ratio of a portfolio that invests in the market portfolio can be improved by also investing in size and value factor portfolios. Thereafter, the evidence has been extended by a profitability and investment factor by Fama and French (2015). This line of research has had a lasting impact on the finance industry. Factor investing is today mainstream, and most major asset management companies offer products with exposure to value, momentum or profitability factors. Frazzini et al. (2018) even showed that the exceptional investment success of Warren Buffet can be largely attributed to the exploitation of the value and profitability in addition to defensive factors.

So far, factor investing sounds promising. Unfortunately, for most factors, the academic literature has yet to provide a good explanation for why they predict positive or negative returns and investors therefore have no good idea of the economic drivers related to a specific factor. Factor investing strategies are thus not well understood and there are several black holes in the academic literature. To give an example, Fama and French favour in their research a risk-based interpretation regarding size and value factors. Small firms and value firms are more likely to go bankrupt during bad times and are subject to distress risk, which can be interpreted as an additional risk factor that matters for specific investors who are particularly concerned about these bad times (very much in the spirit of Merton, 1969, or Mayers, 1973). According to this interpretation, the portfolio advice is as follows: Investors who can bear more of the risks approximated by size and value stocks should tilt their portfolios towards these "factors". What is often overlooked, however, is that this also means that certain investors should turn away from these factors as they want to avoid the additional risks these factors represent. Because the market represents the average investor, and if some investors hold more small firm and value stocks, some other investors must hold less of the same value stocks. Not everyone wants to be a value investor, as pointed out by Cochrane (1999). Fama and French admit that competing interpretations of their empirical results remain viable.

Other authors associate factor returns with irrational behaviour and entertain a mispricing story (Lakonishok et al., 1994).[19] According to such an interpretation, some investors simply overweight popular stocks, while avoiding unpopular stocks. They have non-financial 'taste' for certain stocks that correlate with the size and value characteristics. If so, factor returns are very much a 'free lunch' and all informed investors should engage in factor investing at the expense of the uninformed investors. Moreover, as Shleifer and Vishny (1997) point out, there are 'limits to arbitrage' in practice, and

[19] Daniel and Hirshleifer (2015) for a survey.

exploiting anomalies can be difficult due to high transaction costs and scarce risk capital. Profitable anomalies are then expected to persist, in particular in difficult-to-trade markets.

There are additional arguments, like data mining,[20] that make factor investing less promising. Most importantly, factor investing, according to recent research, appears to destroy itself to some extent. McLean and Pontiff (2016) conducted a meta-study to shed light on this phenomenon. They collected the returns of 97 factor portfolios and provided an in-sample research replication (i.e., they measure performance in the same sample as the original research publication), an out-of-sample research replication (i.e., for a period starting immediately thereafter until the publication date), and post-publication performance information. The results, shown below, suggest that data mining as well as publication-informed trading play a prominent role in practice.

As summarised in Table 3.2, the average performance of the 97 factors drops by 26% 'out-of-sample', which indicates that some factors are likely due to data mining. The post-publication drop is another 32%, and is attributed to publication-informed trading. Some factor returns are quickly exploited by clever investors after they become well-known and, therefore, are unlikely to be due to fundamental risks.

Yet there is an additional headwind for factor investors that comes on top of all of this. Most of the literature and the investment practice report factor returns before taking into account transaction costs. However, some factors require frequent and costly trading. Novy-Marx and Velikov (2016), and Detzel et al. (2023) show that many factor returns are substantially less profitable after taking into account transaction costs. Table 3.3 reports the performance for popular factor portfolios before and after transaction costs,

Table 3.2 Does academic research destroy stock return predictability? (*Source* McLean and Pontiff (2016))

Performance of 97 factor portfolios		
In-sample (replication)	100%	
Out-of-sample	74%	26% vanish due to data mining (upper bound)
Post-publication	42%	32% vanish due to publication-informed trading

[20] Early contributions in this respect are Lo and MacKinlay (1990) and MacKinlay (1995). Recently, Harvey et al. (2013) revived this idea. When thousands of researchers mine the data for successful strategies that outperform the market, per data mining theory, it is inevitable that they eventually find stunning returns even if there are none in reality. Obviously, in this case, investors should not engage at all in factor investing.

Table 3.3 Factor performance before and after accounting for transaction costs. Annualised performance in percentage points. Below 'Gross' is the return before accounting for transaction costs and 'Net' is the return after accounting for transaction costs. 'Change' is the net return divided by gross return minus one. The more negative this number is, the more the factor performance declines after taking into account transaction costs as measured by the bid-ask spread. (*Source* Detzel et al. (2023), results are based on the CRSP/Compustat database from January 1972 to December 2021)

	Gross	Net	Change
Market portfolio	7.56	7.56	0
Size factor	1.68	1.32	−21%
Value factor	3.24	2.64	−19%
Momentum factor	7.68	1.80	−77%
Profitability factor	3.60	2.88	−20%
Investment factor	3.48	2.28	−34%

as provided by Detzel et al. (2023). While the passive market portfolio does not require trading, a factor portfolio requires frequent rebalancing towards stocks with the highest or lowest characteristics. Transaction costs reduce the returns of factor portfolios by between 19 and 77%! In real life, factor portfolio returns are further reduced by additional costs such as brokerage and bank commissions.

In summary, while there is compelling scientific evidence that factor investing can theoretically help investors outperform the simple market portfolio, the net performance achievable from factor investing is likely to be significantly lower than expected. It is also largely unknown what investor should take advantage of which factor, as there is a general lack of an economic foundation on the ultimate drivers behind factors. While the factor investing myth is (usually) not as damaging as the previous fables, there is still plenty of room for disappointment for long-term investors. Before investors consider allocating a portion of their assets to factor strategies, they should be convinced that the expected future risk-adjusted performance, net of fees and transaction costs, is sufficient to improve the performance of a passive portfolio, and they should be convinced that they are not taking on additional risks they are uncomfortable with.

The Performance-Persistence Myth

> The Performance-Persistence Myth in a nutshell: Should investors use past returns to judge an asset? We show that using past performance has almost no value in assessing an investment. We employ empirical evidence to illustrate that past performance chasing is likely not a successful investment strategy.

It is popular amongst investors to judge an asset or a portfolio by looking at its past return over a relatively short period. Actually, the email inbox of the authors is full of investment strategies that come with a fantastic year-to-date performance.

Research has shown that, in particular, non-professional investors seem to form expectations about future asset performance by extrapolating past performance (Greenwood & Shleifer, 2014; Choi & Robertson, 2020). Guercio and Tkac (2008) show this phenomenon for mutual fund investors and document a strong relationship between past performance ratings and mutual fund flows. Such a relationship has been confirmed by many others in the literature (e.g., Ivković & Weisbenner, 2009; Ferreira et al., 2012; Spiegel & Zhang, 2013; Ben-David et al., 2022) with different measures of past performance. In fact, past performance and related fund ratings are among the best predictors of fund flows reported in the literature.

This practice however has at least two flaws. First, past performance is not informative of risk associated with an investment. So while it may be conceivable that a certain fund generated a convincing past return, this number alone says only very little. Without taking risk into account, past returns may simply reflect higher risk rather than better judgement. Risk-adjusting past returns would, therefore, be a minimal requirement for past performance to be a relevant number.

Second, and more importantly, the information contained in past performance numbers has almost no value in assessing an investment. Carhart (1997) show that after appropriately adjusting past mutual fund performance for risk, past performance has no valuable predictive power for future performance. A notable exception in the study by Carhart (1997) are the worst funds in a given year. They indeed continue to perform poorly. Brown and Goetzmann (1995) and Kahn and Rudd (1995) come to the same conclusion, which has since been confirmed by many others.

For illustration, Fig. 3.6 reports the empirical evidence provided by Carhart (1997). At the end of each year from 1962 to 1987, US mutual funds are sorted into ten portfolios based on the past one-year return. The performance of these ten portfolios of mutual funds is then tracked over the following five years. Two things are apparent from the figure. Performance of the top 10% and the flop 10% converge already in the next year to a large extent. The top mutual funds are close in performance to most of their peers and only the worst funds continue to clearly underperform their peers. After accounting for risk, Carhart (1997) finds that even the mild persistence of performance of the top decile mutual funds fully disappears.

Choi and Zhao (2021) find that already the unadjusted past performance does not predict future performance in more recent data that became available after the publication of Carhart (1997). The non-persistence of past investment performance has also been confirmed by Busse et al. (2010) for institutional equity investment mandates and is not confined to mutual funds.

Jagannathan et al. (2010) find more positive evidence on performance persistence for hedge funds. However, a meta-study by Eling (2009) of 25 studies on hedge fund performance persistence finds mixed results depending on the hedge fund database used and the empirical methodology. Due to the varying quality of the underlying data and the fact that it is less clear how

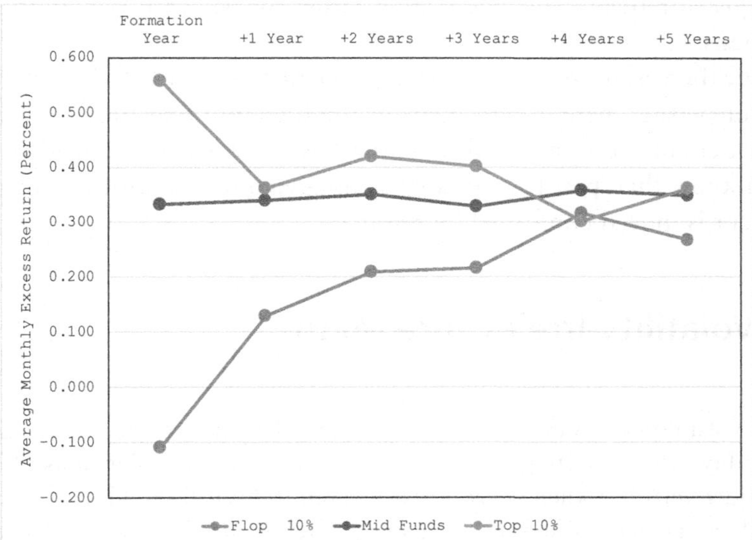

Fig. 3.6 Carhart's evidence on mutual fund performance (non-) persistence. The figure shows the persistence of mutual fund performance from 1962 to 1987. At the end of each year, US mutual funds are sorted into ten portfolios based on the past one-year return. The performance of these ten portfolios of mutual funds is then tracked over the following five years. (*Source* Adapted from Carhart (1997) available at SSRN https://ssrn.com/abstract=8036)

hedge fund returns should be risk-adjusted, it is not possible to draw a clear picture for hedge funds.

The literature mainly discusses two possible reasons why investors chase past returns, even though past performance is not a reliable predictor of future returns. Frazzini and Lamont (2008) argue that mutual fund flows simply reflect 'dumb money'. Under this view, past outperformance is due to chance rather than skill, which is the reason why past performance does not persist into the future. In other words, fund managers basically roll the dice and some will be lucky enough to come up with a high number in a given year. However, the following year, these managers are no more likely to get another high number than the other managers. According to the dumb money hypothesis, investors do not understand that past outperformance is due to luck and thus will likely not be replicated.

Berk and Green (2004), on the other hand, entertain the idea that there is skill in the fund industry and fund flows chase for this skill. However, with more inflows the skilled funds become larger and larger and it becomes increasingly difficult to apply profitable strategies. As a result, the fund size increases over time just until any outperformance disappears. Ben-David et al. (2022) find that fund flows are better explained by simple pasts returns than risk-adjusted returns. This observation rather squares with the dump money hypothesis.

While there is, to some extent, disagreement as to *why* exactly performance does not persist, there is agreement in the literature that fund performance does not endure. You may well recall that most of your financial advisors will let you know that 'past performance is no guarantee for future results'. This statement is indeed confirmed by research.

The Volatility-Irrelevance Myth

> The Volatility-Irrelevance Myth in a nutshell: Many investors do not consider volatility when selecting assets. We show, however, that investors should consider volatility when selecting assets, even if diversified and low volatility portfolios are rarely listed at the top of short-term portfolio rankings. We illustrate the volatility drag on long-term performance, present empirical studies that shed light on the importance of considering volatility when selecting assets, and argue that low-volatility portfolios are likely to shine over longer time-horizons.

Another reason why selecting investments based on short-term performance rankings is bad advice is that such a strategy systematically favours riskier investments over less risky ones. Indeed, higher volatility comes at the expense of long-term performance, as we shall illustrate in this chapter.

The riskier an investment strategy, the higher the variation of realised returns. This means that high-risk strategies end with a higher probability at the top of a short-term performance ranking, even when the expected return is the same as for a low-risk investment strategy. As a result, investors who hunt for investments with high past short-term performance, ignoring volatility, are likely to end up with a more volatile portfolio without better returns. However, in the long run, investments providing a consistent return add up to a higher capital appreciation than more volatile investments that naturally come with more highs, but also more lows. The underlying reason is that more volatile investments must have a larger average return compared to less volatile investments, to win the capital appreciation race over long-horizons.

We illustrate this with an example: A portfolio with a simple return of 5% for three years in a row results in a cumulative three-year return of 15.76% and an average one-year return of 5%.[21] On the contrary, a portfolio earning 20% in year one, 10% in year two and losing 15% also has an average one-year return of 5%. But this series of portfolio returns is more volatile and leads to a lower cumulative three-year return of only 12.20%, even though the second portfolio outperforms in two out of three years.[22] This is because cumulative returns require a greater gain to offset an initial loss. For example, a portfolio of CHF 100 that drops to CHF 50 has an initial loss of 50%. It now requires a return of 100% to offset the initial loss and to climb back to CHF 100. The more volatile a strategy, the more likely it is to suffer a large loss. As a result, for the same arithmetic return, the strategy with the higher volatility will offer a poorer long-term performance.

We further illustrate the volatility drag in Fig. 3.7. We use the annual returns of the diversified global equity and Swiss government bond portfolio from Fig. 2.1 in our next example. In black and in comparison to our Fig. 2.1 portfolio, we scale the return such that the average arithmetic return is unchanged while the volatility is doubled. The Fig. 2.1 portfolio is our low volatility portfolio with an arithmetic annual return of 6.1% (blue bars). The high volatility portfolio with an arithmetic return of 6.1% is shown using black bars. The volatility drag is substantial: the cumulative performance from 1970 to 2013 for an investment of CHF 10,0000 is only CHF 63,100

[21] The calculation is: $[(1 + 0.05) \times (1 + 0.05) \times (1 + 0.05)] - 1 = 0.1576$.

[22] In this case: $[(1 + 0.20) \times (1 + 0.10) \times (1 - 0.15)] - 1 = 0.1220$.

for the high volatility strategy (black bars) compared to CHF 170,600 for the original strategy (blue bars). Volatility thus clearly matters for the long-term performance of an investment strategy.

Picking the portfolio based on the expected Sharpe ratio instead of realised past performance will lead to the consistent selection of the first portfolio and the long-term performance of the blue portfolio in Fig. 3.7. Standard capital market theory thus gives the correct advice, as picking based on short-term performance rankings favours inconsistent strategies with poor long-term performance. We therefore refer to the popular practice of ranking investment strategies by their one-year performance as the 'short-term past performance myth'.

But why is the short-term performance myth popular when it clearly leads to inferior investment performance? One reason is that the relationship between short-term and long-term returns is frequently confused. One can often read the claim that stocks are less risky in the long run, in the sense that the realised return gets closer to the expected return when we simply invest for longer, indicating that risk somehow diversifies over time.

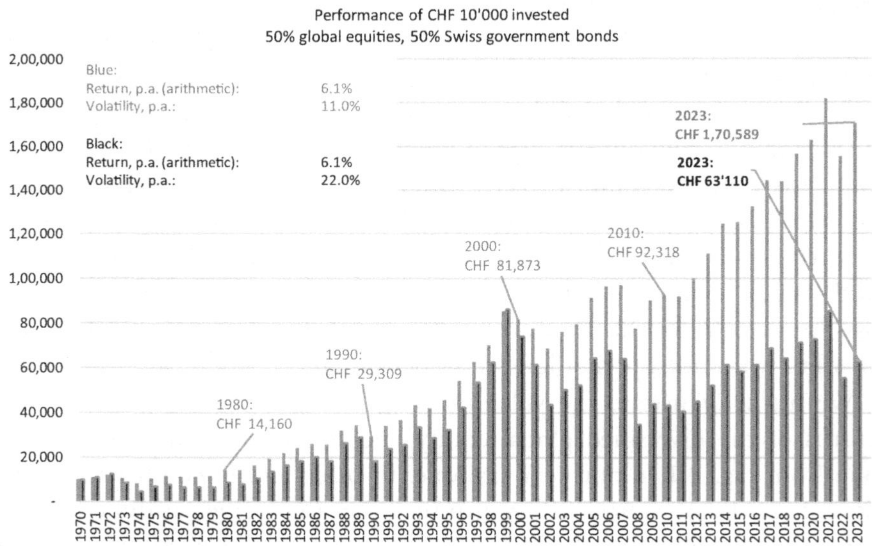

Fig. 3.7 The volatility drag on long-term performance.
The blue portfolio is a diversified portfolio that invests 50% in global equities and 50% in Swiss government bonds, and the results shown are the same as in Fig. 2.1. The black portfolio is a hypothetical portfolio that scales the returns of the diversified portfolio such that it has the exact same average arithmetic return but twice the volatility of the blue portfolio. *Source* MSCI, Pictet, own calculations

According to this logic, the one-year risk is not that important, and performance is all that matters. However, this logic is misleading: As pointed out in 'Samuelson (1963)'s fallacy of large numbers', risk can be diversified in the cross-section only, but not over time. Instead, risk accumulates over time! Two-year returns will come from a wider distribution compared to one-year returns. An investment that is more risky at the one-year horizon is also more risky at the two-year horizon.

Empirical studies on returns achieved over a long period illustrate the impact of time on portfolio returns. Fama and French (2018) propose to re-sample US market portfolio returns to approximate their distribution for an investment horizon of up to thirty years. Anarkulova et al. (2022) replicate such an exercise with international returns. The international sample is plausibly less affected by a selection bias stemming from a single successful market. Indeed, international stocks have performed less favourably than the US market. In Fig. 3.8, we report their main result, the estimated distribution of the final value of one US Dollar invested for a period of 30 years. The distribution of final payoffs is wide, illustrating that the final value of one US Dollar invested is highly uncertain and falls between 0.5 and 23.3 US dollars.[23] These numbers can be compared with the distribution of payoffs from a shorter and one-year investment period. Here, the 5 % percentile is 0.72 (a 28% loss), and the 95 % percentile is 1.49 (a 49% gain). Indeed, a longer investment horizon does not help to reduce risk in terms of dispersion of returns according to the analyses provided by Fama and French (2018) and Anarkulova et al. (2022).

However, the probability of a loss decreases with the investment horizon. Anarkulova et al. (2022) report an estimated probability of a loss at the one-year horizon of 37% and at the 30-year horizon of a lower 12%. The reason is that the distribution of returns not only gets wider over time, but also moves upwards by the average geometric return. As long as the average geometric return is positive, and dependence between one-year returns is not too strong, the probability of a loss must fall over time.

In summary, it is a myth that volatility does not matter for long-term performance. Instead, consistent performance is important for the long-run success of a portfolio. While diversified portfolios rarely appear at the top of the popular short-term portfolio rankings, they are more likely to shine over time.

---

[23] For the 5% percentile, Anarkulova et al. (2022) report a 30-year pay-off of 0.47 (a 53% loss). For the 95% percentile, they report a pay-off of 23.33 (a 2,233% gain).

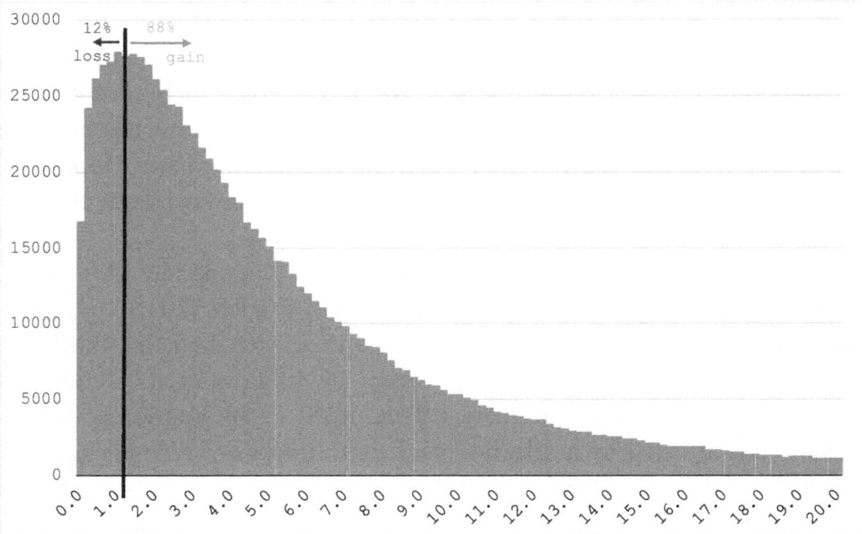

Fig. 3.8 Cumulative 30-year returns.
The figure shows the distribution of the final wealth of one US Dollar that is invested for 30 years. The distribution is from a bootstrap experiment that is based on an empirical sample of international stock returns. (*Source* Adapted from Anarkulova et al. (2022), available at SSRN http://dx.doi.org/10.2139/ssrn.3594660)

The ESG-Investing Myth

The ESG-Investing Myth in a nutshell: We argue against the common belief that sustainable portfolios provide superior performance. We present research that supports the notion that ESG-investments are driven by emotional rather than rational behaviour. We stipulate that asset mispricing due to an ESG (incomplete) information channel and an ESG demand channel may be at work.

ESG-investing refers to investment strategies that consider environmental (E), social (S) and governance (G) aspects. ESG investing has been a strong trend in asset management over the past decade. According to the Global Sustainable Investment Alliance, assets under management in ESG investments amounted to 30 trillion USD in 2022.[24] To bring this number into perspective, the Boston Consulting Group estimates the total market of

[24] Global Sustainable Investment Review 2022, available at https://www.gsi-alliance.org/.

professional asset management at 100 trillion in 2020.[25] The total world-wide public equity and bonds outstanding in 2022 amount to approximately 231 trillion USD according to SIFMA.[26]

In practice, ESG strategies can come in different shades and are based on different investor and fund manager motives. Starks (2023) provides a summary of this industry trend and also shows how mutual funds have shifted their capital towards companies with high ESG ratings over time (Fig. 3.9).

The increasing interest in ESG is striking. Hartzmark and Sussman (2019) show that, after the introduction of the Morningstar sustainability rating, those investment funds that were categorised as being less sustainable recorded net outflows, while funds with high sustainability recorded net inflows. They find evidence that investors' expectations about higher future performance, as well as non-pecuniary motives, are plausible drivers of these fund flows. However, the research on ESG investment strategies[27] is still

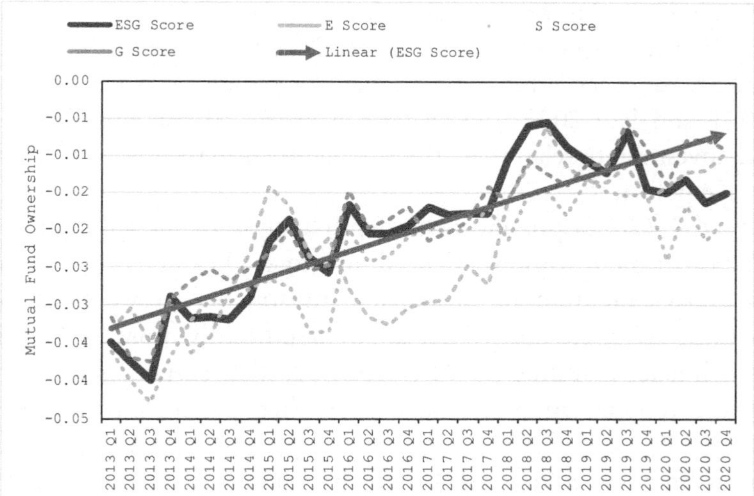

Fig. 3.9 US mutual fund exposure to ESG companies.
The figure shows the difference in active mutual fund ownership in the highest and lowest S&P 500 ESG Score quartiles. Results are shows for the overall ESG Score and the its components. The grey arrow is the linea trend of the ESG Score. (*Source* Adapted from Starks (2023))

[25] Global Asset Management 2021 Report, available at https://www.bcg.com/.

[26] See 2023 Securities Industry and Financial Markets (SIFMA) Capital Markets Fact Book, published in July 2023.

[27] ESG investment strategies include ESG integration, ESG exclusion, ESG best-in-class selection, and impact investing. ESG integration refers to considering ESG-related characteristics when estimating the risk and return of an asset. ESG exclusion strategies drop securities that do not meet certain ESG criteria, while best-in-class strategies pick the securities with the highest ESG score among a

sparse and, from an economic point of view, it seems unlikely that ESG strategies help improve portfolios' long-term financial performance.

Barber et al. (2021) study dual-objective venture capital funds that explicitly commit to achieving positive environmental or social externalities in addition to a financial return. They find evidence that investors of these funds willingly forego some of the financial return, in line with having non-pecuniary motives. Investors with mission objectives and investors who face political pressure have a stronger willingness to pay for 'sustainable investments'. Investors with no such objectives or political pressure (e.g., households, institutions, private pension plans) do not show such a willingness to pay. Barber et al. (2021) find that, on average, investors are willing to accept expected returns on impact investments 2.5–3.7% points lower than market returns, depending on the investor. There seem to be important differences between different groups of investors and their willingness to pay for sustainability. Public pension plans, for example, have a high willingness to pay, while private pension plans have low to none.

According to Giglio et al. (2023), retail investors generally expect ESG investments to underperform the market. According to their study, between mid-2021 and late 2022, the average expected 10-year annualised return of ESG investments relative to the overall stock market was lower by -1.4 percentage points.

Heeb et al. (2022) provide an in-depth analysis of the willingness to pay in a field experiment with experienced investors. They find a substantial willingness to pay a premium for 'sustainable investments'. However, as shown in Fig. 3.10, investors are not willing to pay significantly more for high-impact than low-impact investments. They conclude that sustainable investing "is primarily driven by an emotional, rather than a calculative, valuation of impact".

Gibson Brandon et al. (2022), find that those US institutional investors who are signatories to the Principles for Responsible Investment (PRI) do not have better ESG ratings than non-signatories. The motives for ESG investing are thus not the same for all investors.

The current research findings suggest that non-pecuniary motives are an important driving force behind the ESG investing trend. However, for large parts of the market, these non-pecuniary motives appear to be rather superficial and not impact-oriented.

What then can we expect from ESG investment strategies from a financial performance point of view? Two potential economic mechanisms could

---

peer group. Impact investing refers to investments with a concrete goal to achieve in one or multiple ESG dimensions.

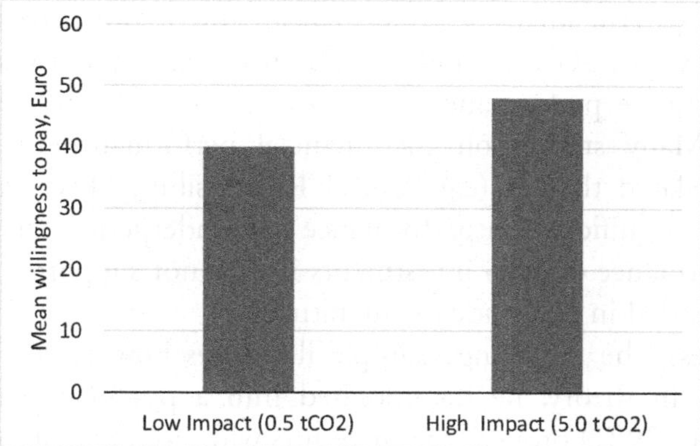

Fig. 3.10 Willingness-to-pay of private investors for "sustainable investments". This figure shows the main result of the field study by Heeb et al. (2022). Private investors are willing to pay for 'sustainable investments' (WTP, depicted on the y-axis), but they are not willing to pay significantly more for a high-impact sustainable investment than a low-impact sustainable investment. (*Source* Heeb et al. (2022) available at SSRN http://dx.doi.org/10.2139/ssrn.3765659)

be at work. First, the ESG information channel. ESG investments could be mispriced, for example, due to incomplete information. In this case, ESG information and its integration into the investment process helps us to identify good deals and help to outperform the market. However, as discussed earlier, the literature on professional asset management finds that experts as a group have a hard time finding mispriced assets in a systematic way (Fama & French, 2010, among many others). Moreover, ESG investing is a trend that has reached mainstream and is on everyone's lips. It seems unlikely that ESG characteristics help to find mispriced assets. Second, the ESG demand channel. A widespread application of ESG exclusion or best-in-class strategies means that specific investors have a strong taste for assets with favourable ESG characteristics. Pástor et al. (2021) and Zerbib (2022) study how taste for green assets affects capital market equilibrium. In line with classic portfolio theory, green assets with high aggregate demand are more expensive than brown assets with low aggregate demand. Accordingly, green assets earn lower expected returns, and portfolios with a green tilt earn lower long-term returns than the market. These are the costs that green investors have to pay to accommodate their tastes. The other side of the medal is that investment costs for green firms become lower, which should be beneficial for green investments. These are the gains from ESG investing.

From an economic point of view, the ESG information channel is unlikely to have a prominent role. Because the ESG demand channel suggests a negative effect, it is more plausible that ESG strategies reduce somewhat a portfolio's long-term financial performance. This is not necessarily bad for ESG investors, as ESG investing serves non-pecuniary motives in exchange for some foregone performance. Empirical evidence broadly confirms this conjecture. Many studies on the financial performance of ESG investments and related themes (e.g., Social Responsibility Investments (SRIs)) find neither a significant outperformance nor underperformance.[28] Systematic outperformance of ESG investments is thus not supported by empirical evidence provided in the academic literature.

Nevertheless, the following example illustrates how such non-pecuniary motives can, in theory, be incorporated into a portfolio relatively easily. Pedersen et al. (2021) propose that investors with non-pecuniary motives can evaluate their portfolio based on the return-risk-responsibility metric, R_p^3. This measure is equal to the traditional Sharpe ratio plus the ESG z-score[29] of the portfolio:

$$R_p^3 = \frac{\mathbb{E}[R_{p,t}] - R_f}{\sigma(R_{p,t})} + \lambda \times ESG_{p,z-score},$$

where $ESG_{z-score,p}$ is the ESG score of the portfolio standard normalised relative to some benchmark. A positive score means that the portfolio does better than the benchmark. λ is investor-specific and captures the willingness to pay for a higher $ESG_{z-score,p}$. For example, a traditional investor might be described by setting $\lambda = 0$, while an ESG investor corresponds by setting $\lambda > 0$. Using the measure appears to be straightforward. The investor calculates the Sharpe ratio of a portfolio and then adds the ESG z-score of the portfolio weighted by λ. If the investor likes ESG a lot and wants to equally weight this criterion with the Sharpe ratio, the weighting factor would be equal to one, $\lambda = 1$). For example, if the portfolio Sharpe ratio is 0.5 and the standardised ESG rating is 1, the R_p^3 measure would amount to 1.5.

In practice, however, investors have to be able to reliably measure the E*th*, S*th*, and G*th* dimensions of an investment. This is easier said than done. Berg et al. (2022) document that ESG ratings disagree to an extent that leaves investors with considerable uncertainty as to how good a firm's ESG

[28] Qualitative literature reviews can be found in Horan et al. (2022), and Matos (2020). Revelli and Viviani (2015) and Hornuf and Yüksel (2023) provide quantitative meta-studies. Some exemplary studies on the relationship between sustainability characteristics and the performance of stocks or mutual funds include Bauer et al. (2005), El Ghoul and Karoui (2017), Gregory et al. (1997), Halbritter and Dorfleitner (2015), Hartzmark and Sussman (2019), Renneboog et al. (2008), and Schröder (2007).

[29] The z-score is a statistical measure describing a value's relationship to the mean of a group of values, expressed in standard deviations from the mean.

performance really is. Furthermore, ESG ratings are also inconsistent over time. Berg et al. (2023) show that ESG rating providers change their ESG scores over time. What has been a good ESG firm in real time in 2020 might become a poor ESG firm with the hindsight of being in the year 2023. Larcker et al. (2023) go so far as to call ESG ratings "a compass without direction".

Taking the academic literature on ESG investing seriously, it appears to be a myth that ESG investing increases long-term returns while having an impact at the same time. "Doing well by doing good" is economically implausible and empirically unfounded. More plausibly, ESG portfolio tilts decrease long-term returns.

Rather than adopting ESG portfolio tilts, such as those found in the best-of-class and exclusion strategies, recent theoretical work suggests that impact investing (Zerbib, 2022) and the introduction of carbon taxes (Pedersen, 2023) are likely to be more efficient paths toward having an ESG impact. Using specific tools to reach separate goals is more promising.

Accordingly, at the individual investor level, an alternative to ESG tilts in the financial portfolio in this sense is first to stick to a traditional, unconstrained ESG investment approach to secure the financial return. However, the benefits of improved financial performance could then be used to donate a greater proportion to charity. Such an approach would be manageable and make it easier to verify the real impact to the greater good that is ultimately achieved.

For the time being (and until more empirical evidence suggests that ESG investing positively impacts portfolio performance), we therefore refrain from using ESG factors to improve financial performance.

References

Akins, B. (2018). Financial reporting quality and uncertainty about credit risk among rating agencies. *Accounting Review, 93*, 1–22.

Anarkulova, A., Cederburg, S., & O'Doherty, M. S. (2022). Stocks for the long run? Evidence from a broad sample of developed markets. *Journal of Financial Economics, 143*, 409–433.

Ardia, D., Guidotti, E., & Kroencke, T. A. (2024). Efficient estimation of bid-ask spreads from open, high, low, and close prices. *Journal of Financial Economics, 161*, Article 103916.

Arrow, K. J. (1971). *Essays in the theory of risk-bearing*. Markham.

Atanasov, V., Møller, S. V., & Priestley, R. (2020). Consumption fluctuations and expected returns. *Journal of Finance, 75*, 1677–1713.

Baker, M., & Wurgler, J. (2000). The equity share in new issues and aggregate stock returns. *Journal of Finance, 55*, 2219–2257.

Bakshi, G., Panayotov, G., & Skoulakis, G. (2011). Improving the predictability of real economic activity and asset returns with forward variances inferred from option portfolios. *Journal of Financial Economics, 100*, 475–495.

Banz, R. W. (1981). The relationship between return and market value of common stocks. *Journal of Financial Economics, 9*, 3–18.

Barber, B. M., Lehavy, R., McNichols, M., & Trueman, B. (2001). Can investors profit from the prophets? security analyst recommendations and stock returns. *Journal of Finance, 56*, 531–563.

Barber, B. M., Morse, A., & Yasuda, A. (2021). Impact investing. *Journal of Financial Economics, 139*, 162–185.

Barber, B. M., & Odean, T. (2000). Trading is hazardous to your wealth: The common stock investment performance of individual investors. *Journal of Finance, 55*, 773–806.

Bauer, R., Koedijk, K., & Otten, R. (2005). International evidence on ethical mutual fund performance and investment style. *Journal of Banking & Finance, 29*, 1751–1767.

Ben-David, I., Franzoni, F., & Moussawi, R. (2017). Exchange-traded funds. *Annual Review of Financial Economics, 9*, 169–189.

Ben-David, I., Li, J., Rossi, A., & Song, Y. (2022). What do mutual fund investors really care about? *Review of Financial Studies, 35*, 1723–1774.

Berg, F., Fabisik, K., & Sautner, Z. (2023). Is history repeating itself? The (un)predictable past of ESG ratings. Working Paper.

Berg, F., Kölbel, J. F., & Rigobon, R. (2022). Aggregate confusion: The divergence of ESG ratings. *Review of Finance, 26*, 1315–1344.

Berk, J. B., & Green, R. C. (2004). Mutual fund flows and performance in rational markets. *Journal of Political Economy, 112*, 1269–1295.

Bessembinder, H. (2018). Do stocks outperform treasury bills? *Journal of Financial Economics, 129*, 440–457.

Bessembinder, H., Chen, T.-F., Chen, G., & Wei, K. C. J. (2023). Long-term shareholder returns: Evidence from 64,000 global stocks. *Financial Analysts Journal, 79*, 33–63.

Bhutta, N., Bricker, J., Chang, A. C., Dettling, L. J., Goodman, S., Hsu, J. W., Moore, K. B., Sarah Reber, A. H. V., & Windle, R. A. (2020). Changes in U.S. family finances from 2019 to 2019: Evidence from the survey of consumer finances. *Federal and Reserve and Bulletin, Board of Governors, 106*, 1–42.

Birchler, U., Volkart, R., Ettlin, D., & Hegglin, R. (2010). Aktienbesitz in der schweiz. Institut für Banking und Finance.

Blume, M. E., & Friend, I. (1975). The asset structure of individual portfolios and some implications for utility functions. *Journal of Finance, 30*, 585–603.

Bollerslev, T., Tauchen, G., & Zhou, H. (2009). Expected stock returns and variance risk premia. *Review of Financial Studies, 22*, 4463–4492.

Bolton, P., Freixas, X., & Shapiro, J. (2012). The credit ratings game. *Journal of Finance, 67*, 85–112.

Boudoukh, J., Michaely, R., Richardson, M., & Roberts, M. R. (2007). On the importance of measuring payout yield: Implications for empirical asset pricing. *Journal of Finance, 62*, 877–915.

Brown, S. J., & Goetzmann, W. N. (1995). Performance persistence. *Journal of Finance, 50*, 679–698.

Busse, J. A., Goyal, A., & Wahal, S. (2010). Performance and persistence in institutional investment management. *Journal of Finance, 65*, 765–790.

Calvet, L. E., Campbell, J. Y., & Sodini, P. (2007). Down or out: Assessing the welfare costs of household investment mistakes. *Journal of Political Economy, 115*, 707–747.

Campbell, J. Y. (2017). *Financial decisions and markets: A course in asset pricing*. Princeton University Press.

Campbell, J. Y. (1987). Stock returns and the term structure. *Journal of Financial Economics, 18*, 373–399.

Campbell, J. Y. (2006). Household finance. *Journal of Finance, 61*, 1553–1604.

Campbell, J. Y., & Shiller, R. J. (1988a). The dividend-price ratio and expectations of future dividends and discount factors. *Review of Financial Studies, 1*, 195–228.

Campbell, J. Y., & Shiller, R. J. (1988b). Stock prices, earnings, and expected dividends. *Journal of Finance, 43*, 661–676.

Cao, S., Jiang, W., Wang, J., & Yang, B. (2024). From man vs. machine to man + machine: The art and AI of stock analyses. *Journal of Financial Economics, 160*, 1–22.

Carhart, M. M. (1997). On persistence in mutual fund performance. *Journal of Finance, 52*, 57–82.

Chen, A. Y., & Zimmermann, T. (2022). Open source cross-sectional asset pricing. *Critical Finance Review, 11*, 207–264.

Choi, N., Fedenia, M., Skiba, H., & Sokolyk, T. (2017). Portfolio concentration and performance of institutional investors worldwide. *Journal of Financial Economics, 123*, 189–208.

Choi, J. J., & Robertson, A. (2020). What matters to individual investors? evidence from the horse's mouth. *Journal of Finance, 75*, 1965–2020.

Choi, J. J., & Zhao, K. (2021). Carhart (1997) mutual fund performance persistence disappears out of sample. *Critical Finance Review, 10*, 263–270.

Cochrane, J. H. (1991). Production-based asset pricing and the link between stock returns and economic fluctuations. *Journal of Finance, 46*, 209–237.

Cochrane, J. H. (1999). Portfolio advice for a multifactor world. *Economic Perspectives, Federal Reserve Bank of Chicago, 23*, 59–78.

Cochrane, J. H. (2008). The dog that did not bark: A defense of return predictability. *Review of Financial Studies, 21*, 1533–1575.

Cooper, M. J., Gulen, H., & Schill, M. J. (2008). Asset growth and the cross-section of stock returns. *Journal of Finance, 63*, 1609–1651.

Cooper, I., & Priestley, R. (2009). Time-varying risk premiums and the output gap. *Review of Financial Studies, 22*, 2801–2833.

Cootner, P. (1964). *The random character of stock market prices*. MIT Press.

Cornaggia, J., & Cornaggia, K. J. (2013). Estimating the costs of issuer-paid credit ratings. *Review of Financial Studies, 26*, 2229–2269.

Cremers, K. M., Fulkerson, J. A., & Riley, T. B. (2019). Challenging the conventional wisdom on active management: A review of the past 20 years of academic literature on actively managed mutual funds. *Financial Analysts Journal, 75*, 8–35.

Cremers, K. J. M., & Petajisto, A. (2009). How active is your fund manager? A new measure that predicts performance. *The Review of Financial Studies, 22*, 3329–3365.

Curcuru, S., Heaton, J., Lucas, D., & Moore, D. (2010). In Y. Ait-Sahalia & L. P. Hansen (Eds.), *Heterogeneity and portfolio choice: Theory and evidence*, Vol. 1, chap. Chapter 6 in the Handbook of financial econometrics: Tools and techniques (pp. 337–382).

Daniel, K., & Hirshleifer, D. (2015). Overconfident investors, predictable returns, and excessive trading. *Journal of Economic Perspectives, 29*, 61–88.

Detzel, A. L., Novy-Marx, R., & Velikov, M. (2023). Model comparison with transaction costs. *Journal of Finance, 78*, 1743–1775.

Dimson, E., Marsh, P., & Staunton, M. (2002). *Triumph of the optimists: 101 years of global investment returns*. Princeton University Press.

Doeswijk, R., Lam, T., & Swinkels, L. (2019). Historical returns of the market portfolio. *The Review of Asset Pricing Studies, 10*, 521–567.

Easley, D., Michayluk, D., O'Hara, M., & Putnins, T. J. (2021). The active world of passive investing. *Review of Finance* 1433–1471.

El Ghoul, S., & Karoui, A. (2017). Does corporate social responsibility affect mutual fund performance and flows? *Journal of Banking & Finance, 77*, 53–63.

Eling, M. (2009). Does hedge fund performance persist? overview and new empirical evidence. *European Financial Management, 15*, 362–401.

Fagereng, A., Gottlieb, C., & Guiso, L. (2017). Asset market participation and portfolio choiceover the life-cycle. *Journal of Finance, 72*, 705–750.

Fama, E. F. (1970). Efficient capital markets: A review of theory and empirical work. *The Journal of Finance, 25*, 383–417.

Fama, E. F., & French, K. R. (1988). Dividend yields and expected stock returns. *Journal of Financial Economics, 22*, 3–25.

Fama, E. F., & French, K. R. (1989). Business conditions and expected returns on stocks and bonds. *Journal of Financial Economics, 25*, 23–49.

Fama, E. F., & French, K. R. (1992). The cross-section of expected stock returns. *Journal of Finance, 47*, 427–465.

Fama, E. F., & French, K. R. (1993). Common risk factors in the returns on stocks and bonds. *Journal of Financial Economics, 33*, 3–56.

Fama, E. F., & French, K. R. (1996). Multifactor explanations of asset pricing anomalies. *Journal of Finance, 51*, 55–84.

Fama, E. F., & French, K. R. (2010). Luck versus skill in the cross section of mutual fund returns. *Journal of Finance, 65*, 1915–1947.

Fama, E. F., & French, K. R. (2015). A five-factor asset pricing model. *Journal of Financial Economics, 116*, 1–22.

Fama, E. F., & French, K. R. (2018). Long-horizon returns. *Review of Asset Pricing Studies, 8*, 232–252.

Ferreira, M. A., Keswani, A., Miguel, A. F., & Ramos, S. B. (2012). The flow-performance relationship around the world. *Journal of Banking & Finance, 36*, 1759–1780.

Florentsen, B., Nielsson, U., Raahauge, P., & Rangvid, J. (2019). The aggregate cost of equity underdiversification. *Financial Review, 54*, 833–856.

Frazzini, A., Kabiller, D., & Pedersen, L. H. (2018). Buffett's alpha. *Financial Analysts Journal, 74*, 35–55.

Frazzini, A., & Lamont, O. A. (2008). Dumb money: Mutual fund flows and the cross-section of stock returns. *Journal of Financial Economics, 88*, 299–322.

Frazzini, A., & Pedersen, L. H. (2014). Betting against beta. *Journal of Financial Economics, 111*, 1–25.

French, K. R. (2008). Presidential address: The cost of active investing. *Journal of Finance, 63*, 1537–1573.

French, K. R., & Poterba, J. M. (1991). Investor diversification and international equity markets. *American Economic Review, 81*, 222–226.

Gârleanu, N., & Pedersen, H. L. (2022). Active and passive investing: Understanding samuelson's dictum. *Review of Asset Pricing Studies, 12*, 389–446.

Gerakos, J., Linnainmaa, J. T., & Morse, A. (2021). Asset managers: Institutional performance and factor exposures. *Journal of Finance, 76*, 2035–2075.

Gibson Brandon, R., Glossner, S., Krueger, P., Matos, P., & Steffen, T. (2022). Do responsible investors invest responsibly? *Review of Finance, 26*, 1389–1432.

Giglio, S., Maggiori, M., Stroebel, J., Tan, Z., Utkus, S. P., Xu, X., & Xu, X. (2023). Four facts about esg beliefs and investor portfolios. SRRN Working Paper.

Goetzmann, W. N., & Kumar, A. (2008). Equity portfolio diversification. *Review of Finance*.

Gomes, F., Haliassos, M., & Ramadorai, T. (2021). Household finance. *Journal of Economic Literature, 59*, 919–1000.

Goyal, A., Welch, I., & Zafirov, A. (2021). A comprehensive look at the empirical performance of equity premium prediction II. Working Paper.

Goyal, A., & Welch, I. (2008). A comprehensive look at the empirical performance of equity premium prediction. *Review of Financial Studies, 21*, 1455–1508.

Greenwood, R., & Shleifer, A. (2014). Expectations of returns and expected returns. *Review of Financial Studies, 27*, 714–746.

Gregory, A., Matatko, J., & Luther, R. (1997). Ethical unit trust financial performance: Small company effects and fund size effects. *Journal of Business Finance & Accounting, 24*, 705–725.

Grinblatt, M., Keloharju, M., & Linnainmaa, J. T. (2011). IQ and stock market participation. *Journal of Finance, 66*, 2121–2164.

Grossman, S. J., & Stiglitz, J. E. (1980). On the impossibility of informationally efficient markets. *American Economic Review, 70*, 393–408.

Grubel, H. G. (1968). Internationally diversified portfolios: Welfare gains and capital flows. *American Economic Review, 58*, 1299–1314.

Guercio, D. D., & Tkac, P. A. (2008). Star power: The effect of monrningstar ratings on mutual fund flow. *Journal of Financial and Quantitative Analysis, 43*, 907–936.

Guiso, L., Sapienza, P., & Zingales, L. (2008). Trusting the stock market. *Journal of Finance, 63*, 2557–2600.

Halbritter, G., & Dorfleitner, G. (2015). The wages of social responsibility - where are they? A critical review of ESG investing. *Review of Financial Economics, 26*, 25–35.

Haliassos, M., & Bertaut, C. C. (1995). Why do so few hold stocks? *Economic Journal, 105*, 1110–1129.

Hartzmark, S. M., & Sussman, A. B. (2019). Do investors value sustainability? A natural experiment examining ranking and fund flows. *Journal of Finance, 74*, 2789–2837.

Harvey, C. R., & Liu, Y. (2022). Luck versus skill in the cross section of mutual fund returns: Reexamining the evidence. *Journal of Finance, 77*, 1921–1966.

Harvey, C. R., Liu, Y., & Zhu, H. (2013). and the cross-section of expected returns. *Review of Financial Studies, 29*, 5–68.

Heeb, F., Kölbel, J. F., Paetzold, F., & Zeisberger, S. (2022). Do investors care about impact? *Review of Financial Studies, 36*, 1737–1787.

Hirshleifer, D., Hou, K., & Teoh, S. H. (2009). Accruals, cash flows, and aggregate stock returns. *Journal of Financial Economics, 91*, 389–406.

Hitzemann, S., Sokolinski, S., & Tai, M. (2022). Paying for beta: Leverage demand and asset management fees. *Journal of Financial Economics, 145*, 105–128.

Horan, S. M., Dimson, E., Emery, C., Blay, K. A., Yelton, G., & Agarwal, A. (2022). *ESG investment outcomes, performance evaluation, and attribution*. CFA Institute Research Foundation: Brief.

Hornuf, L., & Yüksel, G. (2023). The performance of socially responsible investments: A meta-analysis. *European Financial Management* forthcoming.

Hou, K., Xue, C., & Zhang, L. (2015). Digesting anomalies: An investment approach. *Review of Financial Studies, 28*, 650–705.

Ibbotson, R. G., Siegel, L. B., & Lovel, K. S. (1985). World wealth: Market values and returns. *Journal of Portfolio Management, 12*, 4–23.

Ivković, Z., & Weisbenner, S. (2009). Individual investor mutual fund flows. *Journal of Financial Economics, 92*, 223–237.

Jagannathan, R., Malakhov, A., & Novikov, D. (2010). Do hot hands exist among hedge fund managers? An empirical evaluation. *Journal of Finance, 65*, 217–255.

Jank, S. (2015). Changes in the composition of publicly traded firms: Implications for the dividend-price ratio and return predictability. *Management Science, 61*, 1362–1377.

Jegadeesh, N., & Titman, S. (1993). Returns to buying winners and selling losers: Implications for stock market efficiency. *Journal of Finance, 48*, 65–91.

Jorda, O., Knoll, K., Kuvshinov, D., Schularick, M., & Taylor, A. (2019). The rate of return on everything 1870–2015. *Quarterly Journal of Economics, 134*, 1225–1298.

Kahn, R. N., & Rudd, A. (1995). Does historical performance predict future performance? *Financial Analysts Journal, 51*, 43–52.

Kalok Chan, V. C., & Ng, L. (2005). What determines the domestic bias and foreign bias? Evidence from mutual fund equity allocations worldwide. *Journal of Finance, 60*, 1495–1534.

Kaustia, M., Conlin, A., & Luotonen, N. (2023). What drives stock market participation? The role of institutional, traditional and behavioral factors. *Journal of Banking and Finance, 148*, 1–21.

Keim, D. B., & Stambaugh, R. F. (1986). Predicting returns in the stock and bond markets. *Journal of Financial Economics, 17*, 357–390.

Kelly, M. (1995). All their eggs in one basket: Portfolio diversification of us households. *Journal of Economic Behavior and Organization, 27*, 87–96.

Koijen, R. S., & Nieuwerburgh, S. V. (2011). Predictability of returns and cash flows. *Annual Review of Financial Economics, 3*, 467–491.

Kosowski, R., Timmermann, A., Wermers, R., & White, H. (2006). Can mutual fund "stars" really pick stocks? new evidence from a bootstrap analysis. *Journal of Finance, 61*, 2551–2595.

Kumar, A. (2009). Who gambles in the stock market? *Journal of Finance, 64*, 1517–1987.

Lakonishok, J., Shleifer, A., & Vishny, R. W. (1994). Contrarian investment, extrapolation, and risk. *Journal of Finance, 49*, 1541–1578.

Larcker, D. F., Pomorski, L., Tayan, B., & Watts, E. M. (2023). Esg ratings: A compass without direction. Unpublished.

Lettau, M., & Ludvigson, S. (2001). Consumption, aggregate wealth, and expected stock returns. *The Journal of Finance, 56*, 815–849.

Lettau, M., & Nieuwerburgh, S. V. (2008). Reconciling the return predictability evidence. *Review of Financial Studies, 21*, 1607–1652.

Levy, H., & Sarnat, M. (1970). International diversification of investment portfolios. *American Economic Review, 60*, 668–675.

Lewellen, J. (2011). Institutional investors and the limits of arbitrage. *Journal of Financial Economics, 102*, 62–80.

Lewis, K. K. (1999). Trying to explain home bias in equities and consumption. *Journal of Economic Literature, 37*, 571–608.

Li, J., & Yu, J. (2012). Investor attention, psychological anchors, and stock return predictability. *Journal of Financial Economics, 104*, 401–419. Special Issue on Investor Sentiment.

Lim, T. (2002). Rationality and analyst forecast bias. *Journal of Finance, 56*, 369–385.
Linnainmaa, J. T., Melzer, B. T., & Previtero, A. (2021). The misguided beliefs of financial advisors. *Journal of Finance, 76*, 587–621.
Lo, A. W., & MacKinlay, A. C. (1990). Data-snooping biases in tests of financial asset pricing models. *Review of Financial Studies, 3*, 431–467.
MacKinlay, A. C. (1995). Multifactor models do not explain deviations from the CAPM. *Journal of Financial Economics, 38*, 3–28.
Mankiw, N., & Zeldes, S. P. (1991). The consumption of stockholders and nonstockholders. *Journal of Financial Economics, 29*, 97–112.
Markowitz, H. (1952). Portfolio selection. *Journal of Finance, 7*, 77–91.
Martin, I. (2017). What is the expected return on the market? *Quarterly Journal of Economics, 132*, 367–433.
Matos, P. (2020). ESG and responsible institutional investing around the world: A critical review. CFA Institute Research Foundation.
Mayers, D. (1973). Nonmarketable assets and the determination of capital asset prices in the absence of a riskless asset. *Journal of Business, 46*, 258–267.
McLean, R. D., & Pontiff, J. (2016). Does academic research destroy stock return predictability? *Journal of Finance, 71*, 5–32.
Merton, R. C. (1969). Lifetime portfolio selection under uncertainty: The continuous-time case. *Review of Economics and Statistics, 51*, 247–257.
Moskowitz, T. J., Ooi, Y. H., & Pedersen, L. H. (2012). Time series momentum. *Journal of Financial Economics, 104*, 228–250. Special Issue on Investor Sentiment.
Muravyev, D., & Pearson, N. D. (2020). Options trading costs are lower then you think. *Review of Financial Studies, 33*, 4973–5014.
Neely, C. J., Rapach, D. E., Tu, J., & Zhou, G. (2014). Forecasting the equity risk premium: The role of technical indicators. *Management Science, 60*, 1772–1791.
Novy-Marx, R. (2013). The other side of value: The gross profitability premium. *Journal of Financial Economics, 108*, 1–28.
Novy-Marx, R. (2014). Predicting anomaly performance with politics, the weather, global warming, sunspots, and the stars. *Journal of Financial Economics, 112*, 137–146.
Novy-Marx, R., & Velikov, M. (2016). A taxonomy of anomalies and their tradingcosts. *Review of Financial Studies, 29*, 104–147.
Pástor, L., Stambaugh, R. F., & Taylor, L. A. (2021). Sustainable investing in equilibrium. *Journal of Financial Economics, 142*, 550–571.
Pedersen, L. H. (2023). Carbon pricing versus green finance. Working Paper.
Pedersen, L. H. (2018). Sharpening the arithmetic of active management. *Financial Analysts Journal, 74*, 21–36.
Pedersen, L. H., Fitzgibbons, S., & Pomorski, L. (2021). Responsible investing: The ESG-efficient frontier. *Journal of Financial Economics, 142*, 572–597.

Polkovnichenko, V. (2005). Household portfolio diversification: A case for rank-dependent preferences. *Review of Financial Studies, 18*, 1467–1502.
Pratt, J. W. (1964). Risk aversion in the small and in the large. *Econometrica, 32*, 122–136.
Pursiainen, V. (2022). Cultural biases in equity analysis. *Journal of Finance, 77*, 163–211.
Renneboog, L., Ter Horst, J., & Zhang, C. (2008). The price of ethics and stakeholder governance: The performance of socially responsible mutual funds. *Journal of Corporate Finance, 14*, 302–322. Special Issue: Contractual Corporate Governance.
Revelli, C., & Viviani, J.-L. (2015). Financial performance of socially responsible investing (SRI): What have we learned? A meta-analysis. *Business Ethics: A European Review, 24*, 158–185.
Roll, R. (1984). A simple implicit measure of the effective bid-ask spread in an efficient market. *Journal of Finance, 39*, 1127–1139.
Rosenberg, B., Reid, K., & Lanstein, R. (1985). Persuasive evidence of market inefficiency. *Journal of Portfolio Management, 11*, 9–16.
Samuelson, P. A. (1963). Risk and uncertainty: A fallacy of large numbers. *Scientia, 98*, 108–113.
Samuelson, P. A. (1965). Proof that properly anticipated prices fluctuate randomly. *Industrial Management Review, 6*, 41–49.
Schröder, M. (2007). Is there a difference? The performance characteristics of SRI equity indices. *Journal of Business Finance & Accounting, 34*, 331–348.
Sharpe, W. F. (1966). Mutual fund performance. *Journal of Business, 39*, 119–138.
Sharpe, W. F. (1991). The arithmetic of active management. *Financial Analysts Journal, 47*, 7–9.
Shefrin, H., & Statman, M. (2000). Behavioral portfolio theory. *The Journal of Financial and Quantitative Analysis, 35*, 127–151.
Shiller, R. J. (2000). *Irrational exuberance*. Princeton University Press 2000; Broadway Books 2001, 2nd ed., 2005.
Shiller, R. J. (1981). Do stock prices move too much to be justified by subsequent changes in dividends? *American Economic Review, 71*, 421–436.
Shiller, R. J. (2014). Speculative asset prices. *American Economic Review, 104*, 1486–1517.
Shleifer, A., & Vishny, R. W. (1997). The limits of arbitrage. *Journal of Finance, 52*, 35–55.
Spiegel, M., & Zhang, H. (2013). Mutual fund risk and market share-adjusted fund flows. *Journal of Financial Economics, 108*, 506–528.
Starks, L. T. (2023). Presidential address: Sustainable finance and esg issues-value versus values. *Journal of Finance, 78*, 1837–1872.
Tobin, J. (1958). Liquidity preference as behavior toward risk. *Review of Economic Studies, 25*, 65–86.

Welch, I. (2016). The (time-varying) importance of disaster risk. *Financial Analysts Journal, 72*, 14–30.
Zerbib, O. D. (2022). A sustainable capital asset pricing model (S-CAPM): Evidence from environmental integration and sin stock exclusion. *Review of Finance, 26*, 1345–1388.

4

Principles of Evidence-Based Investing

We propose an easy-to-implement 3-portfolio strategy to help investors resist common investment myths. Investors should follow an evidence-based approach by combining three sub-portfolios: (1) the global market portfolio, (2) the alpha portfolio, and (3) the risk-free asset. Implementation is as important as the strategy. Because each sub-portfolio has a specific purpose it can be evaluated by theoretical and empirical evidence. Evidence-based investing is not a one-size-fits-all approach. Investors differ in their preferences and risk tolerance. Evidence-based investing takes these investor-specific differences into account. However, evidence-based investing does not guarantee a specific investment performance. It is an attempt to invest in the best possible way, based on scientific evidence. New scientific evidence is discovered over time and accordingly, investment approaches should be adapted over time.

We have seen that following common investment myths is a poor basis for successful long-term investing. Investors should take a cue from Homer's Odysseus and resist the many temptations offered by financial advisers. The evidence presented suggests that stock picking and market timing do more harm than good, and many complex investment strategies do not actually improve performance after taking transaction costs and management fees into account. So what then should the savvy investor do?

First, we propose an easy-to-implement *3-portfolio strategy* in which investors strategically select from three sub-portfolios (a global market portfolio, an alpha portfolio, and a risk-free asset portfolio). The idea is to simplify the investment process and make it easier to retain control. The strategy can be implemented by everyone, from small to large investors. As each of

P. Böni and T. Kröncke, *The Evidence-Based Investor*,
https://doi.org/10.1007/978-3-031-88675-1_4

the three portfolios has a specific task in the overall portfolio, we can more easily compare the outcomes with our expectations. Second, we emphasise that *disciplined implementation* is as important as the strategy itself. This means that investors are aware of the investment myths, avoid them and use evidence to construct, optimally combine, and frequently evaluate their three sub-portfolios.

The 3-Portfolio Strategy

Academic portfolio theory suggests that we can, in principle, implement an efficient portfolio in two ways. The first approach is to combine hundreds and thousands of individual assets—following the classic approach introduced by Markowitz in 1952. However, as shown by Treynor and Black (1973), there is an elegant alternative. It is also possible to find an efficient portfolio based on a few separate sub-portfolios, each of which has a specific objective. In the following, we will take a closer look at how this approach can be applied to a globally diversified investment portfolio.

The first sub-portfolio is *the global market portfolio* which is well diversified and combines different asset classes and investments across different global regions. The objective of this portfolio is to ensure that the overall portfolio is indeed well-diversified and harvests the return premia that global markets offer. It does generate risk-adequate returns and is the basis for many investors with different risk preferences or even with an appetite for more sophisticated investment strategies. By definition, it does not have the objective of generating an outperformance. Rather the global market portfolio is the benchmark. It sets a hurdle that alternative asset classes and more complex investment strategies must overcome before we consider investing a portion of the overall portfolio in them. The global market portfolio utilises low-cost passive investment vehicles such as index funds or ETFs wherever possible.

This brings us to the second sub-portfolio: *the alpha portfolio*. This is where the investor focuses on investment opportunities that will help her to further improve performance. The alpha portfolio comprises alternative asset classes (e.g., private market funds allocating capital to private equity, private debt, infrastructure, and real estate) or investment strategies (e.g., quantitative strategies, discretionary strategies, or hedge funds) which, when added to the global market portfolio, help to improve the performance of the investor's overall portfolio. The alpha portfolio may also be fitted to individual investor preferences in respect to the liquidity of assets, or hedging demands for non-financial risks. Investments in the alpha portfolio may justify higher fees than the passive investments contained in the global market portfolio. Importantly, these investments deliver alpha net of fees.

The final step is to manage the absolute risk of the overall portfolio using *the risk-free asset*. The global market portfolio combined with the alpha portfolio may provide an attractive return relative to the risk taken. However, the absolute risk can still be too high for certain individual investors. In this case, the addition of the risk-free asset to the mix allows an investor to reduce the absolute amount of risk without affecting the relative return per unit of risk taken.

But what are the main advantages of splitting the portfolio into three sub-portfolios? Note that each of the sub-portfolios has a different, though clearly defined objective. As such, they can be evaluated (and adjusted) based on how well they meet that objective. For example, the global market portfolio aims to be well diversified and to capture global multi-asset risk premia. The alpha portfolio aims to further improve the performance of the global market portfolio, while the risk-free asset limits the absolute amount of risk taken. Such objectives are measurable and help the investor to assess them over time. This, in turn, is the basic prerequisite for a disciplined investment approach.

Disciplined Implementation

Rather than investing based on beliefs and feelings, evidence-based investing relies on facts and logical consistency. Investors must avoid being seduced by investment advisers who promote strategies that have no track record of improving the portfolio. Like Odysseus who tied himself to a mast to avoid being driven off course by the Sirens, investors should refrain from allocating capital to the investment myths described above.

As we have seen, short-term performance is notoriously noisy and a poor predictor of long-term investment performance. Instead of evaluating short-term past investment results, evidence-based investing evaluates the causes of past, as well as, expected future performance. Moreover, not all empirical evidence is equally useful. It is important that empirical findings stand the test of time and that we have a theory that makes what we observe logically plausible.

Adaptive Tailored Approach

Evidence-based investing must be tailored to individual investors' preferences and is not simply a one-size-fits-all approach. First, the absolute risk must be adjusted to an investor's risk tolerance. Second, the composition of the alpha portfolio should be investor-specific. Some investors might be uncomfortable with illiquid investments, assets that co-move with labour or entrepreneurial income, or brown stocks. Rather than investing according to the preferences of advisors or a one-dimensional target, evidence-based investing tailors portfolios towards the heterogeneous preferences of investors. Third, evidence-based investing is a scientific approach to allocating capital to promising asset classes and investment strategies. An essential characteristic of science is that old hypotheses about how the world works are discarded over time due to the advent of new, more convincing findings. Investment hypotheses must therefore be re-evaluated and the fit of the overall investment strategy with an investor's preferences must periodically be re-validated. Is, for example, an investor's risk appetite still the same as one year ago? In the case of a retail investor, risk tolerance might depend on life stages. So a young investor, say in his or her 30s or 40s, may have a risk tolerance which diverges from that of an investor in his 50s or 60s. In the case of an institutional investor, changing asset and liability management (ALM) considerations must also be taken into consideration. In this sense, evidence-based investing is, at each point in time, an effort to enact the most favourable portfolio given the current state of knowledge and prevailing preferences. Hence, both the state of investment knowledge and investor preferences must be re-evaluated and adapted over time.

How can we then build a 3-portfolio strategy and implement a more disciplined, adaptive, and tailored investment approach? There are several practical challenges to overcome. However, overcoming them is not as difficult as it may first appear. Let us first discuss how we could build the first of our three portfolios, *the global market portfolio* in the next chapter.

Reference

Treynor, J. L., & Black, F. (1973). How to use security analysis to improve portfolio selection. *Journal of Business, 46*, 66–86.

5

The Global Market Portfolio

The global market portfolio is diversified across liquid asset classes and geographical regions. It can be implemented using low-cost passive mutual funds or exchange-traded funds. How to actually combine different asset classes remains an open question. The textbook approach of weighting asset classes by market capitalisation is critically assessed and alternatives such as fixed weights ("60/40") and GDP-based weights are discussed. What they all have in common is that they do not take into account political and economic developments. In response, we present a novel approach that takes into account institutional consensus expectations on the performance of different asset classes to construct a global market portfolio, guided by empirical evidence.

As illustrated in Chapter 3, portfolio theory recommends that investors interested in financial performance should maximise the Sharpe ratio of their portfolios. Recall that the Sharpe ratio is defined as the expected risk premium of a portfolio divided by the expected risk. Intuitively, by maximising the Sharpe ratio, investors are trying to get the most out of the risk they are taking. The 'efficient' portfolio is an allocation that achieves the objective of maximising the Sharpe ratio of the portfolio, although it is difficult to find in practice. As explained in section "A First Step Towards Efficient Portfolios", a global market portfolio is much simpler to build but is likely to be already in the neighbourhood of the efficient portfolio and, importantly, can be used as an elementary first step in building an efficient portfolio. Accordingly, the global market portfolio is the fundamental component of our 3-portfolio strategy.

P. Böni and T. Kröncke, *The Evidence-Based Investor*,
https://doi.org/10.1007/978-3-031-88675-1_5

Implementing the global market portfolio requires some understanding of how market portfolios are constructed in practice today. In sections "The Value-Weighted Global Market Portfolio" and "Criticism of the Value-Weighted Global Market Portfolio", we argue that practical problems arise in a multi-asset context because the value-weighted portfolio—the traditional proxy for a market portfolio—is dominated by government bonds, and the demand from large institutional investors would lead to an implausible mix of asset classes.

Several alternatives to the value-weighted multi-asset market portfolio can be found in investment practice, as we shall see in section "Alternatives to Value-Weights", but they also have important shortcomings. Either they are rule-based, with fixed weights, and thus cannot take account of the macroeconomic and political environment, or else they are discretionary, allowing for an *ad hoc* response to new developments. However, such discretionary approaches tend to be driven by gut feelings, often leading to underperformance. Ideally, we would like to have a rule-based approach, one that takes both macroeconomic factors and the political environment into account!

We have, therefore, devised a novel, yet simple approach, one that is evidence and rule-based at the same time and explained in detail in sections "A Global Market Portfolio Guided by Empirical Evidence" and "Implementation of a Global Market Portfolio Guided by Institutional Capital Market Assumptions". The starting point is the observation that the capital market assumptions of institutional investors continuously reflect the evolution of macroeconomic and political developments and their potential impact on financial markets. By translating these developments into quantitative figures such as the expected return and risk of different asset classes, a rule-based methodology for constructing a global market portfolio can be derived.

As we will see, building such a global market portfolio is less difficult than one might think. Moreover, we will illustrate how a well-diversified global market portfolio outperforms a portfolio consisting of only Swiss bonds and Swiss equities but first, let us start with some basics.

A First Step Towards Efficient Portfolios

In his seminal paper, Markowitz (1952) presents the algorithm that enables one to find efficient portfolios. This approach is still taught to finance students today. As anticipated by Markowitz himself, however, it has proved extremely difficult to apply the algorithm to find efficient portfolios in the real world.

The main issue is not the algorithm by itself, but that we know so little about the necessary ingredients. Investors have to estimate the future *expected return and expected risk* of thousands of financial assets. However, each estimate will be a combination of an asset's true objective expected return and estimation noise. It is exactly this estimation noise which causes the trouble. The Markowitz algorithm turns out to heavily favour those assets with large positive estimation noise. As a result, optimised portfolios overweight the 'lucky' assets and not necessarily the 'right' ones (Britten-Jones, 1999; Cochrane, 2007). Such portfolios optimised over lucky assets using past data are then likely to perform poorly in the future and this has indeed been confirmed in the academic literature (DeMiguel et al., 2009). In the end, Markowitz portfolio optimisation fails in practice, not because the concept is bad, but because the necessary ingredients are not directly observable and can only be approximated with substantial uncertainty.

Some 60 years ago, Sharpe (1964), Lintner (1965) and Mossin (1966) presented a simplifying shortcut when they independently derived the famous Capital Asset Pricing Model (CAPM). It turns out that if all investors followed the advice of Markowitz (1952) and all held risky assets in proportion to the efficient portfolio, each could effectively free-ride on the others without any optimisation or any knowledge of the expected returns or risks. A short thought experiment illustrates the idea. Consider a market in which all investors hold an efficient portfolio. Since the aggregate demand for assets (i.e., the portfolios of individual investors) must equal the aggregate supply of assets (the market value of all assets in the economy), it follows that the efficient portfolio is equal to the 'value-weighted' portfolio that simply adds up all assets. Such a portfolio is called the 'market portfolio'. Therefore, if the Sharpe-Lintner-Mossin description of the world is sufficiently accurate, the market portfolio will have the best possible risk/return ratio and is also the most 'efficient' portfolio. So instead of optimising their portfolio, investors could also invest directly in the market portfolio!

However, an investor-specific adjustment might be necessary. An efficient market portfolio could come with too much risk from the perspective of a given investor. In this case, the combination of the market portfolio with a risk-free asset can be used to manage the absolute risk (Tobin, 1958). All portfolios that combine the risk-free asset with the efficient market portfolio will have the same Sharpe ratio. Investors have different risk preferences and will, therefore, choose different combinations, thereby managing the absolute amount of risk. The greater the weight of the risk-free asset, the lower the overall portfolio risk and the more stable the future path of the invested assets.

This principle is illustrated in Fig. 5.1. The market portfolio is assumed to have the maximum possible Sharpe ratio (which equals the slope of the black line) and is, therefore, the efficient portfolio of risky assets. Investors can decrease (or increase) the absolute amount of risk by combining the efficient market portfolio (green dot), with the risk-free asset (grey dot), as indicated by the black line. All combinations of these two sub-portfolios will have the same Sharpe ratio but they will differ in the amount of absolute risk and return they offer.

Of course, in the real world, the market portfolio may not be efficient, as opposed to the figure, and we will discuss this in more detail in Chapter 6. It could, therefore, be plausibly a little more to the right and slightly lower (i.e., lying inside the curve drawn and not perfectly tangential), so its Sharpe ratio is not the highest possible. However, given its simplicity, the market portfolio is still a good starting point and a solid foundation for constructing more sophisticated portfolios. In fact, in the following chapter, we explain how investors can begin with the market portfolio and then add a second

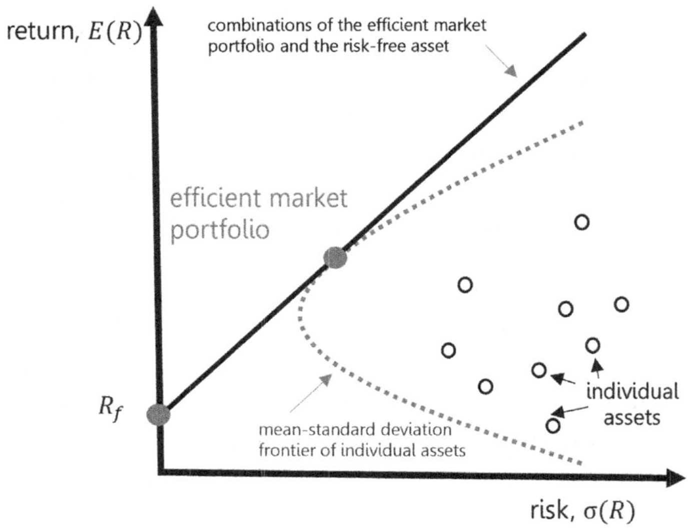

Fig. 5.1 Combining the efficient market portfolio with the risk-free asset. This figure shows how optimal portfolios can be found by combining the efficient market portfolio (green dot) and the risk-free asset (grey), illustrated by the black line. Each combination will have the same Sharpe ratio, which is equal to the slope of the black line. Own illustration (Color figure online)

portfolio to get closer to the efficient portfolio. However, we first need to discuss some of the key practical challenges associated with investing in a global market portfolio.

The Value-Weighted Global Market Portfolio

In theory, the market portfolio is a value-weighted portfolio that simply adds up all individual assets and can be calculated at any time for financial assets. Indeed, for narrowly defined asset classes, such as publicly traded Swiss stocks, it is certainly possible to construct and invest in such a portfolio (e.g., ETFs that track market indices). But such a portfolio would be too narrow for what we are seeking, as other countries and asset classes are excluded!

What we mean by the global market portfolio is a multi-asset portfolio that invests globally. In order to obtain a global market portfolio that is closer to its theoretical counterpart, it would be necessary to aggregate investments across different asset classes and around the world. In practice, unfortunately, this portfolio is neither observable nor investable, as famously pointed out in Roll (1977)'s critique. Many assets are privately owned and therefore impossible for everyone to invest in.

A common workaround to this problem is limiting 'the market' to that which is observable and investable, primarily publicly traded financial assets (Stambaugh, 1982). Doeswijk et al. (2014) provide an estimate of the composition of the global market portfolio with multiple asset classes. A data update by the authors for the year 2023 is shown in Fig. 5.2.

According to Doeswijk et al. (2014), the value-weighted global market portfolio attributes 43% to global equities, 24% to global government bonds, and 15% to global corporate bonds. The remaining 18% of the portfolio comprises inflation-linked bonds, emerging market debt, high-yield bonds, real estate, and investable private equity. Doeswijk et al. (2014) provide annual updates of their estimates, which do not change much over time.[1] The value-weighted multi-asset market portfolio is filled with low-yielding bonds. Unsurprisingly, such a multi-asset market portfolio is rarely implemented in practice.

[1] Other research comes to similar numbers. MSCI (2024) estimate the global market portfolio at the end of 2022. It is composed of 53.1% global fixed income, 38% global equity, 3.3% listed real estate and listed infrastructure, and 5.6% of investable private markets.

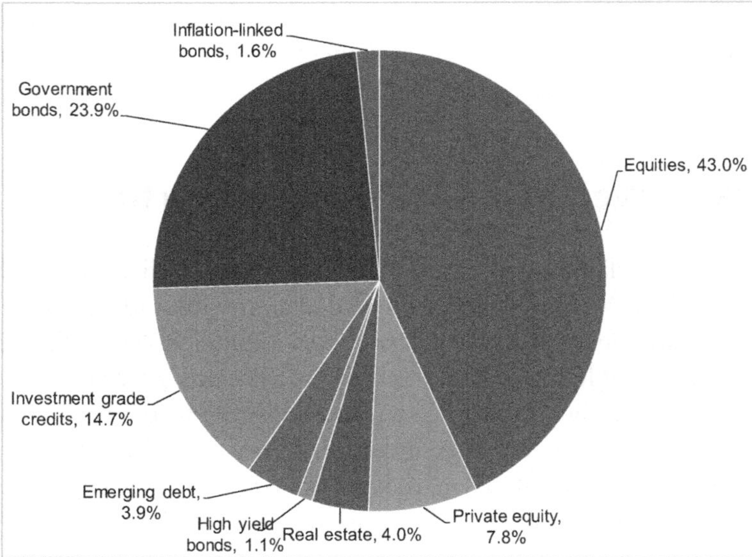

Fig. 5.2 The global market portfolio at the end of 2023. This figure illustrates the composition of a global market portfolio following Doeswijk et al. (2014). The figure is adapted from the data update provided by the authors available at https://doi.org/10.25397/eur.9371741.v6

Criticism of the Value-Weighted Global Market Portfolio

We believe it is right that investors do not blindly invest in and become hooked on the notion of a value-weighted multi-asset portfolio. Such a portfolio in actual fact does not fully reflect the market portfolio as theorised by Sharpe (1964), Lintner (1965), and Mossin (1966). This is because the CAPM is a theory that rests on a set of simplified assumptions, i.e., the CAPM in its basic form only holds in an idealised world.[2]

More realistically, many assets are private and not everyone can invest in them. Moreover, private assets potentially introduce a bias into the observable public market portfolio, making it inefficient, even if the 'true market' were efficient (Roll, 1977). In addition, all investors are supposed to take the prices of financial assets as a given, whereas real-life observations suggest that several very large investors (such as governments, central banks, and large

[2] The main assumptions underlying the CAPM are that (i) Investors are risk averse and evaluate their investment portfolios based on expected return and risk as measured over a single holding period. (ii) Capital markets are perfect, which means that all investors take prices as given and have access to the same investment opportunities. (iii) Investors make the same assumptions about future returns, risks, and the correlation of assets.

institutional investors) influence or affect the prices of publicly traded assets. Governments, for example, may issue large amounts of debt beyond what would be feasible in a competitive market (Jiang et al., 2021), while central banks buy and sell large quantities of financial assets with the explicit aim of influencing their prices and achieving their particular monetary policy (e.g., Bernanke, 2020; Krishnamurthy & Vissing-Jorgensen, 2011). Large institutional investors, such as pension funds and investment funds, can also influence the pricing of certain assets as they shift from one asset class to another (e.g., Gabaix & Koijen, 2022; Haddad et al., 2021). They may do so for purely regulatory reasons (Jansen, 2023), without any intention of optimising the return/risk trade-off. As a result, certain asset classes may be over- or under-represented in the value-weighted proxy of the market portfolio relative to a hypothetical competitive market counterpart.

Alternatives to Value-Weights

The problem of the over- or under-representation of certain asset classes in the observable market portfolio relative to the ideal competitive market portfolio could be addressed in various ways. A first option to adjust for over- or under-representation is to simply adjust the value-weighted market portfolio by the aggregate holdings of central banks and other very large investors that potentially affect asset prices. However, this ignores the precept that demand should affect the valuation of assets and, therefore, ultimately the expected returns of asset classes (Pástor et al., 2021). For example, if central banks buy 50% of all government bonds, the act of reducing the weighting of government bonds by the corresponding amount in the multi-asset market portfolio will not take into account that the expected return on the remaining government bonds is also negatively affected by the demand effect created.

A pragmatic alternative to avoid over- or under-representation is to limit certain asset classes in the multi-asset market portfolio by applying fixed weights. This alternative is frequently used in practice. An example is the classic 40/60 portfolio (composed of 40% bonds and 60% equities). Constructing a portfolio based on fixed weights has some merits. Blake et al. (1999), Arshanapalli et al. (2001), and Annaert et al. (2005) find that fixed weights market portfolios perform favourably compared to discretionary allocations of institutional investors. Perhaps more importantly, the simplicity of fixed weights market portfolios allows for a relatively straightforward implementation. However, fixed portfolio weights are based on a heuristic and cannot take any developments in the global capital markets into account.

For example, if a 40/60 fixed weights investor observes a high demand from central banks or pension funds for government bonds so that the expected return falls, the investor holding a fixed weights market portfolio cannot take this information into account.

Another approach is to weight markets according to the economic characteristics of different markets. For example, Jacobs et al. (2014) argue that some countries have less developed capital markets than others, while countries with well-developed capital markets could therefore be systematically over-represented in the value-weighted market portfolio. Jacobs et al. (2014) suggest weighting the contribution of a particular country by GDP to allow better diversification across regions. However, we would like to stress that listed companies are often global companies with a relatively modest contribution to the GDP of a particular country in which they are listed. Therefore, using GDP weights does not necessarily allow for better diversification across countries.

Against this background of alternative approaches, it is not surprising that discretionary asset allocations remain popular in practice. They allow exposure to certain asset classes to be limited while taking into account fundamental developments in capital markets. The shortcoming of the discretionary approach is that it typically relies on a small sample of experts who might be subject to biased viewpoints. Led by opinions, feelings, and emotions, a discretionary approach may lead to extreme allocations that have little in common with a well-diversified global market portfolio.

We have therefore developed a novel and relatively simple-to-implement evidence and rule-based alternative approach to portfolio construction, one which can overcome the shortcomings of the typical multi-asset portfolios described above.

A Global Market Portfolio Guided by Empirical Evidence

Historical data are often extrapolated to obtain expectations on the attractiveness of a specific asset class. However, given the market- and price distortions created by large investors such as governments, central banks, and large institutional investors, historical data alone are not well suited to obtaining meaningful expectations of future returns and risks. Due to their backwards-looking nature, purely historical estimates will likely not take into account anticipated changes in policies (of governments and central banks) or anticipated macroeconomic changes that will often lead very large institutional investors to reallocate assets and thereby influence asset prices. Instead, *forward-looking estimates* are better suited to managing a global market portfolio. They rest on the currently available information to plausibly account for political and macroeconomic changes.

We propose the use of a forward-looking approach to determine the weighting of asset classes within a global market portfolio, thereby tilting the portfolio towards more attractive asset classes while avoiding the optimisation pitfalls discussed above. To this end, we start from either a value-weighted or a fixed-weighted market portfolio. To be clear, the evidence-based weight of asset class i is given by:

$$w_{i,\text{evidence-based}} = w_{i,\text{basis}} + w_{i,\text{adjustment}},$$

where $w_{i,\text{basis}}$ is the weight of a basis portfolio that could be a traditional value-weighted or a fixed-weighted market portfolio. The adjustment term $w_{i,\text{adjustment}}$ takes empirical forward-looking evidence into account. If such evidence suggests that, for example, government bonds are currently unattractive and represent a slack in the basis portfolio ($w_{i,\text{basis}}$), the weighting is adjusted accordingly and reduced ($w_{i,\text{adjustment}} < 0$). The question now is how to arrive at meaningful (forward-looking) expectations and thus determine the adjustment term $w_{i,\text{adjustment}}$.

The academic literature does not provide a simple answer. Asset pricing models could be used in principle. However, they are inherently simplified versions of the real world and are expected to be imperfect (Campbell, 2017). Even if one uses asset pricing models, which one of the various asset pricing models should be used? Another option is to rely on the opinion of experts, although some experts will prefer different models, and may even use different input data to derive forward-looking capital market expectations. Disagreement among experts concerning their expected returns and risks for different asset classes stems from such disagreements.

A simple method that has been successfully applied in economics and finance in the presence of model uncertainty is model averaging (see, e.g., the surveys provided by Steel, 2020; Timmermann, 2006). The idea we apply to our problem is to average across multiple forward-looking expert estimates (coming from different models) and to obtain an average forward-looking estimate of the expected return and risk of different asset classes. While not a guarantee for the best possible prediction, model averaging is based on a broad consensus, thereby avoiding extreme outsiders' views of the world. So let us shed some light on how an evidence-based global market portfolio can be implemented in the next section.

Implementation of a Global Market Portfolio Guided by Institutional Capital Market Assumptions

How can one implement a global market portfolio that is guided by empirical evidence? We illustrate how this can be achieved within three steps. The first step is to collect institutional long-term capital market assumptions across different asset classes and to consolidate the expectations across many institutions. In the second step, a rule-based methodology is developed to find the adjustment term that takes the consolidated institutional long-term capital market assumptions into account. The third step sets limits on the adjustment to ensure that the asset allocation remains in line with investor preferences. We next discuss a possible implementation of this approach with concrete numbers.

Step I. We collected the expected return and risk for thirteen different asset classes from capital market assumption reports published by 19 asset managers and consultants (specifically Swiss Government Bonds, Corporate Bonds, High-Yield Bonds, Equities US, Equities Europe ex Switzerland, Equities Switzerland, Equities Japan, Equities Pacific ex Japan, Equities Emerging Markets, REITs Global, inflation-linked bonds, commodities, and gold). The choice of asset classes is motivated by the availability of capital market assumptions as well as investable instruments such as ETFs. We use the latter to track the performance of different strategies in the following analysis. At the same time, we target to cover a wide range of asset classes (bonds, equities, liquid alternatives) as well as our potential exposure to all investable regions in the world.

Long-term capital market assumption reports are periodically published by institutional asset managers and consultants to guide their clients concerning their asset allocation decisions. Recent academic research has documented two features of institutional capital market assumptions that we consider utterly important. First, as Dahlquist and Ibert (2023) show, they are counter-cyclical, in line with the present-value relationship and dynamic asset pricing models (Bansal & Yaron, 2004; Campbell & Cochrane, 1999; Campbell & Shiller, 1988a; Fama & French, 1988; Wachter, 2013). In contrast to the expectations of households, they do not simply extrapolate past performance and instead take fundamentals into account. This means that institutional expectations are in their dynamic time-series behaviour consistent with finance theory.

Second, as evidenced by Couts et al. (2023), long-term capital market assumptions come with a reasonable risk-return relationship. Asset classes with higher systematic risk thus earn higher expected returns. This means that they are also in the cross-section of assets, again consistent with finance theory.

However, capital market expectations show considerable heterogeneity in the reported numbers, reflecting not only the usage of different asset pricing models but also the usage of different information and judgement calls. We consolidate our capital market assumptions following Timmermann (2006) and Steel (2020) by relying on the median expectations across the different institutions for a given asset class. If, for example, the consolidated expectations indicate that Swiss government bonds are relatively unattractive, we then utilise this information to derive a downward adjustment for $w_{i,\text{adjustment}} < 0$.

Step II. In this next step, we take the heterogeneity between capital market experts into account when constructing the adjustment term, $w_{i,\text{adjustment}}$. Expert predictions can be in close agreement or else come with large disagreement. Intuitively, if expectations align among a group of experts, the signal is more informative. For example, if all available expert opinions agree on the expected return of bonds being depressed in the long run, there is likely to be some truth in it, and the signal is highly informative. On the other hand, if some experts are optimistic about Japanese stocks, while others are pessimistic, the signal on Japanese stocks is likely less informative. We solve this challenge by drawing from the Black-Litterman model (Black & Litterman, 1991, 1992), and using the information that expert disagreements convey in constructing our portfolio weights.

In addition to accounting for expert disagreement, we also aim to avoid market timing. We do this by imposing a constraint to keep the systematic risk of the evidence-based market portfolio, relative to the basis portfolio, constant. This results in portfolio tilts that are based on the relative attractiveness of different asset classes, rather than asset classes becoming more or less aggressive in absolute terms. For example, the portfolio is more likely to tilt between different bond or equity markets than between bonds and equities. Our approach is thus in line with empirical evidence provided by Goyal and Welch (2008) and Goyal et al. (2021), which suggests that market timing the equity premium is difficult in practice.

Step III. We then limit the maximum and minimum possible values of the adjustment term $w_{i,\text{adjustment}}$. This final step is necessary, as the disagreement-weighted consolidated capital market assumptions will still be subject to some estimation error that could lead to a very large or very small allocation to certain asset classes if implemented aggressively (Britten-Jones, 1999; Couts et al., 2023; DeMiguel et al., 2009). Investors typically specify minimum and maximum bands for asset classes, and we can directly make use of them for this purpose. If the benchmark allocation for government bonds, for example, is 15%, then the minimum and maximum allocation might be set between 10% and 20%. Such bands can be interpreted as a prior on the expected reasonable variation of the impact of the capital market assumptions on the asset allocation. These bandwidths help to limit the impact of the consolidated capital market assumptions on the asset allocation.

We provide a concrete implementation of a global market portfolio, guided by institutional capital market assumptions. In Table 5.1. At the end of 2023, we collected the long-term capital market assumptions of 19 asset managers and consultants, including BlackRock, StateStreet, JP Morgan, and AON, *inter alia*, for 13 global asset classes and cash, as reported in the table. The horizon of the expectations is ten years, or the closest horizon reported. As capital market expectations are typically presented in US dollars, we have first converted them into Swiss Francs, adjusting for the interest rate differential and assuming a fully currency-hedged position. The expectations shown in Table 5.1 are consolidated by taking the cross-sectional median across institutions for each asset class.

Several interesting observations can be made. The highest consolidated expected return is observed for equities in the Pacific region *ex Japan* (8.7%) and Emerging Markets (8.6%), while gold comes with a low expected return of just 1.3%. In terms of risk, equities in Emerging Markets come with the highest expected standard deviation of 20.8%, while Swiss government bonds and (investment grade) corporate bonds have the lowest standard deviation with 5.5% and 6.4%, respectively. However, individual expectations can deviate quite substantially from the median. In the column 'Disagreement', we report the cross-sectional standard deviation of the expected return across the available capital market assumptions. Disagreement tends to be stronger for equity markets relative to bond markets. For example, equities in Japan come with the largest disagreement of 2.5%, followed by equities in Europe *ex Switzerland* with 2.2%. Assuming a normal distribution, about 95% of institutional expert opinions for equities Japan will be in the interval 2.7%–12.7%, and for equities Europe *ex Switzerland* in the interval 2.7%–11.5%. The variation of expected returns between institutional experts is as large as the variation of risk premia over time according to the literature (Campbell & Shiller, 1988b; Cochrane, 2011). In contrast to the equity markets, all four bond markets (Swiss government bonds, corporate bonds, high-yield bonds, and inflation-linked bonds) show a disagreement of around

Table 5.1 A global market portfolio guided by institutional capital market assumptions. This table shows a global market portfolio guided by institutional capital market assumptions. The first three columns show the asset class, median expected return, E(R), and median expected risk, Std(R), of up to 19 institutional capital market assumptions (e.g., BlackRock, StateStreet, JP Morgan, AON, and 15 others) at the end of 2023. The next column shows the 'disagreement' on expected returns, measured as the cross-sectional standard deviation of institutional return expectations. On the right-hand side of the table are the pre-specified weights of a basis portfolio, $w_{i,\text{basis}}$. In the last column are the evidence-based weights of a global market portfolio that take into account the institutional capital market assumptions, the disagreement, and the weights of the basis portfolio to overweight attractive and underweight unattractive asset classes, $w_{i,\text{evidence-based}}$.

Asset class	E(R), %	Std(R), %	Disagr., %	$w_{i,\text{basis}}$	$w_{i,\text{evidence-based}}$
Swiss government bonds	1.8	5.5	1.2	15.0	10.0
Corporate bonds	3.0	6.4	1.0	10.0	15.0
High-yield global	5.1	10.0	1.0	5.0	10.0
Equities US	5.8	16.9	1.4	30.0	24.3
Equities Europe ex Switzerland	7.1	17.4	2.2	7.5	4.5
Equities Switzerland	7.6	13.7	1.2	5.0	5.3
Equities Japan	7.7	16.4	2.5	2.5	1.3
Equities Pacific ex Japan	8.7	19.6	1.6	2.5	4.4
Equities emerging markets	8.6	20.8	1.7	2.5	4.4
REITs global	6.1	18.9	2.2	5.0	9.5
Inflation-linked Bonds	2.6	7.0	0.8	5.0	7.3
Commodities	3.8	16.5	1.3	5.0	2.1
Gold	1.3	14.5	1.2	5.0	2.0
Cash, CHF	1.3	0.0			

1.0 %. Put differently, experts are more in alignment regarding the attractiveness of bond markets than equity markets or riskier liquid alternatives such as REITs and commodities.

The column '$w_{i,\text{basis}}$' gives the weights of a hypothetical pre-specified basis portfolio. This portfolio is illustrative and can be replaced by a different (well-diversified) asset allocation. On the far right, in the column labelled '$w_{i,\text{evidence-based}}$', are the weights of a portfolio that incorporates the capital market assumptions in the manner described above. To do this, the expected Sharpe ratio is maximised based on the expected return and risk characteristics according to the capital market assumptions, while the deviation from the initial basis portfolio is down-weighted in proportion to the degree of disagreement. The result is a well-diversified global market portfolio reflecting a consolidated forward-looking view of the relative attractiveness of different markets.

It is important to understand the importance of a forward-looking view: Suppose that central banks around the world begin to buy high-yield bonds to stimulate investment, thereby depressing the expected return on this asset class. Forward-looking capital market assumptions will reflect such a policy change and the weighting of high-yield bonds will consequently be reduced. The global market portfolio guided by institutional capital market assumptions incorporates structural shifts in the return/risk trade-off for long horizons. By construction, the potential benefits of such a portfolio tilt are unlikely to materialise in the short term, given that the signal is slow-moving and only captures fundamental changes in capital markets.

But what if there are absolutely no such fundamental changes in the capital markets? While unlikely over a longer period, this remains theoretically possible. The result would be that an optimised portfolio would not need many adjustments from quarter to quarter. In such a scenario, the tilts implied by the capital market assumptions would be small and the performance differential necessarily tiny. This is a feature and not a bug. By analogy, when we go to the doctor for a routine check-up and it turns out that we are actually very healthy, we would not want to undergo major surgery and so nothing needs to be done. Nevertheless, it would be silly not to have regular check-ups just because everything has been fine up until now. The benefit of a regular 'portfolio check-up', based on capital market assumptions, is to be prepared for cases where the expected return or risk of certain asset classes change and require your attention.

However, there is also a psychological benefit to regular 'portfolio check-ups'. They can help investors feel confident about a globally diversified portfolio and stay invested in the most promising asset classes, even during times of market stress and high uncertainty. Moreover, capital market assumptions help us not to focus much on short-term past performance which, as we have seen above, provides flawed information which is unhelpful when making asset allocation decisions.

So how do the weights of different asset classes in the evidence-based global market portfolio vary over time? Based on institutional capital market assumptions from 2016 through 2023 and a quarterly portfolio rebalancing, we can answer this question in Fig. 5.3. The figure shows the time-varying portfolio weights of the 13 asset classes over time. Note the following observations: First, our approach reduces the weight of gold in the portfolio after the COVID-19 pandemic, as its prices rose to new all-time highs during the crisis. Apparently, institutional asset managers and consultants considered gold to be expensive, limiting the potential for future expected returns. Second, the overall allocation to bonds is relatively stable over time and the portfolio frequently shifts between government and corporate bonds. Third, there are several shifts between commodities and inflation-linked bonds, and between REITs and global equity markets. Overall, these results are consistent with the objective of tilting the cross-section towards more attractive asset classes, while at the same time avoiding changes in the overall risk-taking, for example by shifting heavily between bonds and equities.

Figure 5.4 provides the performance of the global market portfolio as guided by institutional capital market assumptions. The performance is compared with two alternative and frequently implemented portfolios. First, a home-biased portfolio invested 50% in Swiss government bonds and 50% in Swiss equities. Second, a simple global portfolio invested 50% in Swiss government bonds and 50% in global equities (MSCI World). The performance of the three portfolios is also tabulated in Table 5.2.

From 2016 to 2023, the guided global market portfolio ranks first in terms of cumulative performance with a gain of 47.7%. Over the same period, the simple global portfolio, where equity weights are value-weighted according to the MSCI World Index, would have added 31.7% to an investor's capital, while the home-biased portfolio gained a lower 25.2%. In terms of mean (arithmetic) returns, the guided global market portfolio generated an annual

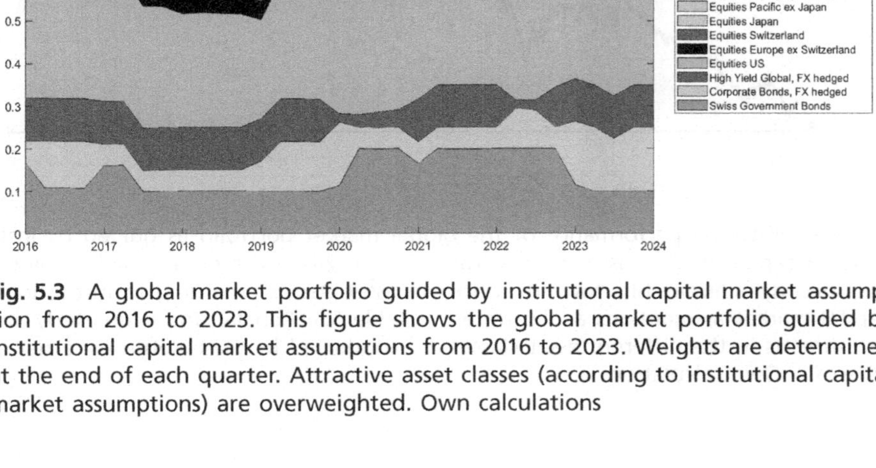

Fig. 5.3 A global market portfolio guided by institutional capital market assumption from 2016 to 2023. This figure shows the global market portfolio guided by institutional capital market assumptions from 2016 to 2023. Weights are determined at the end of each quarter. Attractive asset classes (according to institutional capital market assumptions) are overweighted. Own calculations

return of 5.5%, followed by the simple global portfolio (3.9%), and the home-biased portfolio (3.3%).

The evolution over time also illustrates important characteristics of the guided global market portfolio and the two alternatives proposed. In 2020, all three portfolios were associated with large losses in the first months of the COVID-19 pandemic. In fact, none of them are examples of risk-on/risk-off (market-timing) strategies that could plausibly avoid such sudden downturns. Instead, they all remain invested throughout. Nevertheless, all three portfolios achieved reasonable capital appreciation over longer time horizons, despite the pandemic backlash in 2020 and rising interest rates in 2022, both of which negatively impacted bond and equity prices. Finally, the global market portfolio guided by institutional capital market assumptions outperforms the other approaches over the period considered. Given the stability of the weightings over time, as discussed above, this is primarily achieved by diversifying across 13 global asset classes and achieving broader diversification as compared to the other two narrower counterparts.

The global market portfolio guided by institutional capital market assumptions thus appears to be attractive, not only from a performance perspective. The investor always knows why some assets are divested while others are acquired. The increase and decrease of asset classes in the allocation results

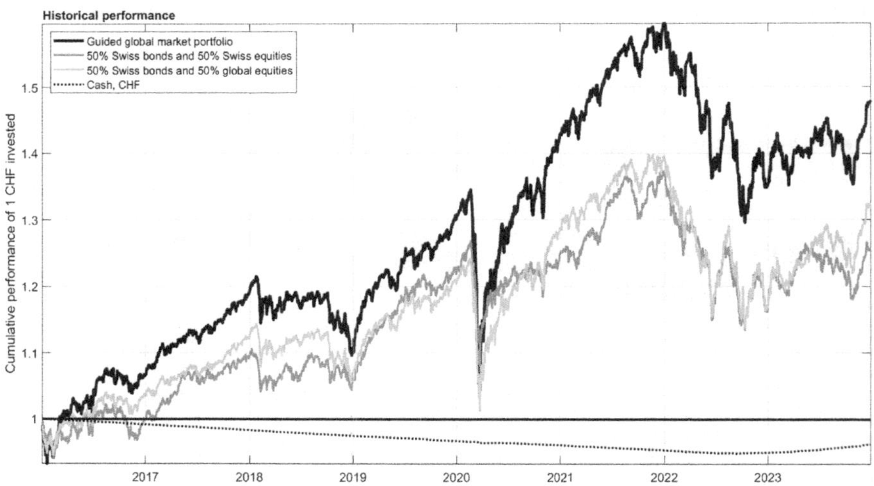

Fig. 5.4 Historical performance of the global market portfolio as guided by institutional capital market assumptions from 2016 to 2023. The guided global market portfolio dynamically tilts towards attractive asset classes according to institutional capital market assumptions as illustrated in Table 5.1. Rebalancing is quarterly and investments in the different asset classes are conducted by ETFs. Returns are net of ETF-costs. Own calculations

Table 5.2 Historical performance of the global market portfolio as guided by institutional capital market assumptions. This table reports the annual return of three portfolios that invest from the beginning of 2016 until the end of 2023. The 'guided global' market portfolio dynamically tilts towards attractive asset classes according to institutional capital market assumptions as illustrated in Table 5.1. "Swiss 50/50" invests 50% in Swiss government bonds and 50% in Swiss equities. "Global 50/50" invests 50% in Swiss government bonds and 50% in global equities (MSCI world). The rebalancing is quarterly and the investments in the different asset classes are approximated by ETFs. There are no other costs considered beyond the costs deducted from the ETFs

Year	Guided Global, %	Swiss 50/50, %	Global 50/50, %
2016	6.6	0.0	3.6
2017	11.5	9.1	8.2
2018	−6.8	−3.4	−4.6
2019	17.4	15.6	12.6
2020	9.8	2.5	6.9
2021	11.8	9.7	8.5
2022	−15.3	−15.2	−16.4
2023	9.3	7.7	12.8
Mean arithmetic	5.5	3.3	3.9
Mean geometric	5.0	2.8	3.5
Cumulative	47.7	25.2	31.7

from a rules-based approach that uses a large number of institutional capital market assumptions as input, rather than the gut feeling of a small subset of advisors.

However, as we illustrated above, while important, this portfolio is only one of three portfolios we need to consider as part of our 3-portfolio strategy. As we will now show, investing additionally in the alpha portfolio (this chapter) may improve the attractiveness of our approach further.

References

Annaert, J., De Ceuster, M. J., & Van Hyfte, W. (2005). The value of asset allocation advice: Evidence from the economist's quarterly portfolio poll. *Journal of Banking & Finance, 29*, 661–680.

Arshanapalli, B. G., Coggin, T. D., & Nelson, W. B. (2001). Is fixed-weight asset allocation really better? *Journal of Portfolio Management, 27*, 27–38.

Bansal, R., & Yaron, A. (2004). Risks for the long run: A potential resolution of asset pricing puzzles. *Journal of Finance, 59*, 1481–1509.

Bernanke, B. S. (2020). The new tools of monetary policy. *American Economic Review, 110*, 943–983.

Black, F., & Litterman, R. (1991). Asset allocation combining investor views with market equilibrium. *Journal of Fixed Income, 1*, 7–18.

Black, F., & Litterman, R. (1992). Global portfolio optimization. *Financial Analysts Journal, 48*, 28–43.

Blake, D., Lehmann, B. N., & Timmermann, A. (1999). Asset allocation dynamics and pension fund performance. *Journal of Business, 72*, 429–461.

Britten-Jones, M. (1999). The sampling error in estimates of mean-variance efficient portfolio weights. *The Journal of Finance, 54*, 655–671.

Campbell, J. Y. (2017). *Financial decisions and markets: A course in asset pricing*. Princeton University Press.

Campbell, J. Y., & Cochrane, J. H. (1999). By force of habit: A consumption-based explanation of aggregate stock market behavior. *Journal of Political Economy, 107*, 205–251.

Campbell, J. Y., & Shiller, R. J. (1988a). The dividend-price ratio and expectations of future dividends and discount factors. *Review of Financial Studies, 1*, 195–228.

Campbell, J. Y., & Shiller, R. J. (1988b). Stock prices, earnings, and expected dividends. *Journal of Finance, 43*, 661–676.

Cochrane, J. H. (2007). Portfolio theory. Supplementary Chapters to *Asset pricing*.

Cochrane, J. H. (2011). Presidential address: Discount rates. *Journal of Finance, 66*, 1047–1108.

Couts, S. J., Gonçalves, A. S., & Loudis, J. A. (2023). *The subjective risk and return expectations of institutional investors* (Working Paper).

Dahlquist, M., & Ibert, M. (2023). *Equity return expectations and portfolios: Evidence from large asset managers* (Working Paper).

DeMiguel, V., Garlappi, L., & Uppal, R. (2009). Optimal versus naive diversification: How inefficient is the 1/n portfolio strategy? *Review of Financial Studies, 22*, 1915–1953.

Doeswijk, R., Lam, T., & Swinkels, L. (2014). The global multi-asset market portfolio, 1959–2012. *Financial Analysts Journal, 70*, 26–41.

Fama, E. F., & French, K. R. (1988). Dividend yields and expected stock returns. *Journal of Financial Economics, 22*, 3–25.

Gabaix, X., & Koijen, R. S. J. (2022). *In search of the origins of financial fluctuations: The inelastic markets hypothesis* (Working Paper).

Goyal, A., & Welch, I. (2008). A comprehensive look at the empirical performance of equity premium prediction. *Review of Financial Studies, 21*, 1455–1508.

Goyal, A., Welch, I., & Zafirov, A. (2021). *A comprehensive look at the empirical performance of equity premium prediction II* (Working Paper).

Haddad, V., Moreira, A., & Muir, T. (2021). When selling becomes viral: Disruptions in debt markets in the Covid-19 crisis and the fed's response. *Review of Financial Studies, 34*, 5309–5351.

Jacobs, H., Müller, S., & Weber, M. (2014). How should individual investors diversify? An empirical evaluation of alternative asset allocation policies. *Journal of Financial Markets, 19*, 62–85.

Jansen, K. A. E. (2023). *Long-term investors, demand shifts, and yields* (Working Paper).

Jiang, Z., Lustig, H., Van Nieuwerburgh, S., & Xiaolan, M. (2021). *The U.S. public debt valuation puzzle* (Working Paper).

Krishnamurthy, A., & Vissing-Jorgensen, A. (2011). *The effects of quantitative easing on interest rates: Channels and implications for policy*. Brookings Papers on Economic Activity 2011.

Lintner, J. (1965). The valuation of risk assets and the selection of risky investments in stock portfolios and capital budgets. *Review of Economics and Statistics, 47*, 13–37.

Markowitz, H. (1952). Portfolio selection. *Journal of Finance, 7*, 77–91.

Mossin, J. (1966). Equilibrium in a capital asset market. *Econometrica, 34*, 768–783.

MSCI. (2024). *On the global market portfolio, private-equity markets and Chinese public-equity markets*. Report for the Norwegian Ministry of Finance.

Pástor, L., Stambaugh, R. F., & Taylor, L. A. (2021). Sustainable investing in equilibrium. *Journal of Financial Economics, 142*, 550–571.

Roll, R. (1977). A critique of the asset pricing theory's tests Part I: On past and potential testability of the theory. *Journal of Financial Economics, 4*, 129–176.

Sharpe, W. F. (1964). Capital asset prices: A theory of market equilibrium under conditions of risk. *Journal of Finance, 19*, 425–442.

Stambaugh, R. F. (1982). On the exclusion of assets from tests of the two-parameter model: A sensitivity analysis. *Journal of Financial Economics, 10*, 237–268.

Steel, M. F. J. (2020). Model averaging and its use in economics. *Journal of Economic Literature, 58*, 644–719.

Timmermann, A. (2006). Forecast combinations. In G. Elliott, C. Granger, & A. Timmermann (Eds.), *Handbook of economic forecasting* (Vol. 1, 1st ed., Chap. 04, pp. 135–196). Elsevier.

Tobin, J. (1958). Liquidity preference as behavior toward risk. *Review of Economic Studies, 25*, 65–86.

Wachter, J. A. (2013). Can time-varying risk of rare disasters explain aggregate stock market volatility? *Journal of Finance, 68*, 987–1035.

6

The Alpha Portfolio

> The alpha portfolio combines alternative asset classes and active investment strategies based on theoretical and empirical evidence. Backed by a strong rationale for economic mechanisms likely driving outperformance, the alpha portfolio improves the performance of the global market portfolio. We emphasise that investors need to consider a potential mispricing in financial markets, and consciously think about priced but not yet considered risk factors when selecting assets for the alpha portfolio. Moreover, they must continually gather and evaluate empirical evidence on the performance of alpha opportunities. Does the observed (net of cost) performance match ex-ante expectations? The alpha portfolio is combined with the global market portfolio to achieve the highest expected return in excess of the risk-free asset, given a certain risk preference.

The global market portfolio alone, while attractive, is unlikely to offer the highest possible expected Sharpe ratio. Rather, it is plausible that there are additional investments that, when combined with the global market portfolio, will further improve the Sharpe ratio of the overall portfolio. Such additional investments are referred to as 'alpha' opportunities and will be allocated to the second of our three portfolios, hereafter referred to as the 'alpha portfolio'. To find the 'efficient' portfolio, an investor has to finally *combine* the global market portfolio with the alpha portfolio (Treynor & Black, 1973).

However, the challenge of building an alpha portfolio is a familiar one. Just as expected returns are inherently difficult and fuzzy to measure, alphas are no easier to quantify. We believe that investors who want to identify true alpha opportunities must ask themselves two important questions: (i) What is

P. Böni and T. Kröncke, *The Evidence-Based Investor*,
https://doi.org/10.1007/978-3-031-88675-1_6

the economic mechanism leading to an alpha opportunity? (ii) Is there strong empirical evidence supporting the idea that there is persistent and significant alpha to be earned? Searching for alpha, when properly executed, is not a simple task. So let us dive deeper into this topic in the following section.

Searching for Alpha

Alpha refers to a measure of performance that was first studied in detail by Jensen (1968). For the asset class or investment strategy i, the alpha with respect to the market portfolio m can be expressed as:

$$\alpha_i = (\mathbb{E}\left[R_{i,t}\right] - R_f) - \beta_i \times (\mathbb{E}\left[R_{m,t}\right] - R_f),$$

where β_i is the beta of an asset within the market portfolio. If we are convinced that the alpha is positive, $\alpha_i > 0$, adding the investment strategy (or asset class) i to the market portfolio is expected to increase the Sharpe ratio of the overall portfolio.

To explain the equation a little more precisely, the element $\beta_i \times (\mathbb{E}\left[R_{m,t}\right] - R_f)$ gives the expected return of asset i according to the Capital Asset Pricing Model (CAPM). If the market portfolio is indeed efficient (i.e., it achieves the maximum Sharpe ratio), then the expected return can be determined by the beta of an asset such that alpha is zero ($\alpha_i = 0$) for all assets.

For investors, the more interesting case arises when the alpha is not zero. If the expected return, according to the CAPM, is lower than the actual expected return, the alpha is positive ($\alpha_i > 0$). Accordingly, the market portfolio is inefficient and the efficient portfolio requires investing a little more in asset i relative to the market. A negative alpha ($\alpha_i < 0$) would suggest that the efficient portfolio requires investing a bit less in asset i compared to the market.

This means that we can use the market portfolio as a benchmark to gauge additional (more sophisticated) investments. But what if an investor is actually not invested in 'the market' portfolio? This is not a problem. We can still use the exact same approach to gauge whether we should add a given investment to the current portfolio. In this case, the market portfolio m would have to be replaced by the investor's current portfolio, which becomes now the relevant benchmark.

The concept is thus simple. In the next step, we collect alpha investments and build an alpha portfolio. As shown by Treynor and Black (1973), investors can combine such an alpha portfolio with the market portfolio to obtain an efficient portfolio. As before, the efficient portfolio can now be combined with the risk-free asset to reduce the overall risk of the efficient portfolio and to match the risk-taking preference of a particular investor. We illustrate this idea in Fig. 6.1. So, instead of two sub-portfolios, we now have to decide how to allocate investments between three sub-portfolios .[1]

The figure illustrates another important result of portfolio theory. There are at least two different ways to find the efficient portfolio. First, one could combine the market portfolio and the alpha portfolio to find the efficient portfolio. This approach is derived from Treynor and Black (1973). However, lending from Markowitz (1952), one could also combine, in a single step, the individual assets to find the same efficient portfolio. While the traditional Markowitz approach is better known, we believe that the Treynor and Black (1973) approach produces more resilient portfolios in practice.

First, dealing with sub-portfolios is simply more practical than dealing with thousands of individual assets. The global market portfolio can be standardised and managed cost-effectively. The alpha portfolio, in contrast, can reflect investor-specific preferences and considers individual tastes for specific

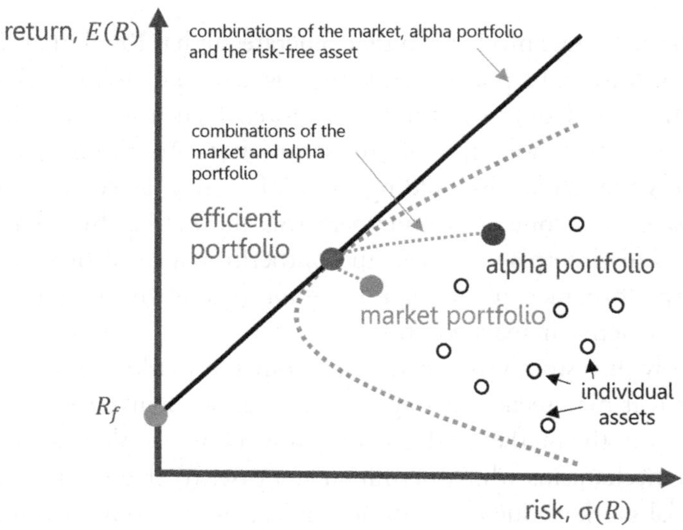

Fig. 6.1 Combining the market portfolio, the alpha portfolio, and the risk-free asset to obtain efficient portfolios. An efficient portfolio (blue dot) can be found by combining the market portfolio (green dot) and the alpha portfolio (violet dot). Optimal portfolios then combine the efficient portfolio with the risk-free asset (grey), illustrated by the black line. Each combination will have the same Sharpe ratio, which is equal to the slope of the black line. Own illustration (Color figure online)

[1] Such an approach is often referred to as core-satellite portfolio management (e.g., Singleton, 2004). The core can be thought of as the market portfolio and the satellites as the alpha opportunities.

sophisticated investment strategies. For the investor, what really matters is the alpha net of costs and not absolute costs. So, in general, alpha strategies that offer larger alphas can justify larger fees just so long as the alpha, net of fees, remains positive and economically relevant.

Second, the (global) market portfolio is a benchmark that additional investments have to pass. An alpha investment opportunity should be judged on its contribution to the overall portfolio, measured in terms of alpha (net of fees) and not its isolated return. The former is usually a higher bar to clear. Based on alphas, we can directly test empirically, using historical data or forward-looking expectations, whether there is a real improvement in a portfolio's Sharpe ratio. Such a hurdle adds a layer of caution to the investment process as it helps an investor to think about the economic mechanism that allows an asset class or investment strategy to improve the performance of a well-diversified benchmark portfolio.

The Economic Mechanisms Underlying Alpha

What is the economic mechanism that generates alpha? Recall that the market portfolio, at least in its pure form, is the aggregate portfolio of all investors. This means that if one investor holds more of an asset than the market, someone else must hold less of the same asset. Accordingly, if someone outperforms the market by holding more of a given asset then, conversely, there must be someone who underperforms the market by holding less of that asset. This interplay between the outperformance of one investor and the underperformance of another is famously known as Sharpe (1991)'s arithmetic of active management.

Obviously, investors want to deviate from the market in the 'right' way and, at first, it may seem puzzling as to why another investor would choose to deviate from the market in the 'wrong' way. However, there are at least two economic mechanisms which permit such a case: (i) there is a mispricing in the financial markets due to investment mistakes by certain investors, or (ii) there is a lack of demand for certain assets for rational reasons.

Mispricing in financial markets rests on the idea that one group of investors can outsmart another. Of course, everyone in asset management would like to claim to be 'smarter' than his or her competitors. However, as illustrated by the investment myths discussed earlier, our knowledge so far suggests that it is unlikely that investors can consistently identify and exploit asset mispricing in modern financial markets. The risk inherent in active trading is that a supposedly mispriced asset is not actually mispriced at all, or that the degree of mispricing is insufficient to profit from after deducting transaction costs. Cochrane (2022) describes this as follows: "When having dinner with lions, make sure you are at the table not on the menu".

Another potential source of alpha is the lack of demand for certain assets. Some investors may, for some entirely rational reason, dislike specific assets with specific characteristics. It is then plausible that those investors who hold more of these unpopular assets than the average investor will be compensated with 'alpha' and a higher Sharpe ratio of their overall portfolio.

A concrete example is that many investors want to avoid illiquid assets. Illiquid assets are harder to sell quickly at their fair price and thus many investors dislike such assets because of their need for a high degree of liquidity or even for regulatory reasons. If the average investor prefers to hold less illiquid assets in exchange for more liquid assets, there will be an overall lack of demand for the illiquid assets. Long-term investors may be less concerned about liquidity and may step in if they are appropriately compensated. As a result, it is plausible that illiquid assets offer a premium in terms of alpha to compensate those willing to hold such assets within their portfolios.

Based on this intuition, Amihud and Mendelson (1986), provide a theoretical justification for an illiquidity premium in financial markets. More recent research confirms this for the case of bond investors. According to Chen et al. (2022), active investors, like mutual funds, have a preference for high-liquidity bonds as these can be easily liquidated during times of market stress. In contrast, passive institutional investors have a preference for less liquid assets in order to receive an illiquidity premium.

So let's have a look at some asset classes and investment strategies that are commonly believed to deliver alpha with respect to a market portfolio of financial assets. Table 6.1 provides a non-exhaustive overview. The list includes private equity, private debt, direct real estate, infrastructure, cryptocurrencies, factor investing, discretionary investing, and hedge funds.[2]

Starting with private debt, there are strong reasons to believe that alpha is available for this asset class. Increased regulation since the Global Financial Crisis of 2007 often makes it unattractive or even impossible for borrowers to rely upon traditional banking channels or public markets. According to Chernenko et al. (2022), a large fraction of non-bank lending can be attributed to bank regulations that constrain banks' ability to lend. As Block et al. (2023) show, private debt funds provide cash flow-based loans and can thus finance companies and provide levels of leveraging that banks can no longer support in view of the increased regulation. Private debt funds profit from this fact,

[2] Ilmanen (2011, 2022) provide detailed investigations of various alpha sources that go beyond those we report in Table 6.1.

Table 6.1 Alpha: Economic mechanism and empirical evidence. This table provides an overview of alternative asset classes and investment strategies that are commonly believed to generate alpha relative to a market-wide portfolio of financial assets. Under 'Economic mechanism', a potentially plausible economic mechanism as a source of alpha is listed. Under 'Empirical evidence' we give an indication of the strength of the empirical evidence for the existence of alpha. In brackets, we list selected publications that we consider representative of the literature. It is not possible to provide an accurate assessment of all the literature within this table, and our assessment may thus be deemed selective

Strategy	Economic mechanism?	Empirical evidence? (Selected research)
Alternative asset classes:		
Private debt	Specialness, capital recycling	Strong (e.g., Böni & de Roon, 2023; Böni & Manigart, 2023; Cumming et al., 2019)
Private equity	Selection skill, illiquidity	Mixed (e.g., Franzoni et al., 2012; Kaplan & Schoar, 2005; Phalippou & Gottschalg, 2008)
Direct real estate	Asset class, illiquidity	Strong (e.g., Jorda et al., 2019; Kallberg et al., 1996; Martin Hoesli & Witkiewicz, 2004)
Crypto	New technology, scarcity	Unknown, due to lack of long history (e.g., Harvey et al., 2022)
Investment strategies:		
Factor investing	Mispricing, demand channel	Mixed (e.g., Detzel et al., 2023; McLean & Pontiff, 2016; and references in section "Empirical Evidence on Alpha")
Discretionary investing	Mispricing	Weak (e.g., Barber & Odean, 2000; Barber et al., 2008; Fama & French, 2010; and references in section "Empirical Evidence on Alpha")
Hedge funds	Mispricing, demand channel, access to arbitrage opportunities	Mixed (e.g., Ackermann et al., 1999; Kosowski et al., 2007; Malkiel & Saha, 2005)

and target unleveraged returns that appear to be high relative to their risk. While divergent from the bank loan market and the syndicated loan market, private debt markets share certain characteristics with them. Private debt funds are special in the sense that they deliver more flexible capital solutions to borrowers.

Theoretically, outperformance is explained by the 'special' nature of private debt funds and the willingness of borrowers to pay for this 'specialisation'. Böni and de Roon (2023) provide an additional argument as to why private debt funds are able to provide alpha. They present evidence that the active trading of debt positions during the early life of a fund (the so-called capital recycling during the investment phase of a fund) likely generates alpha. According to the authors, the alpha of private debt funds amounts to an annualised 8.2% during a private debt fund's early lifetime although this more than halves to 3.9% during the late stage of a fund's life, given its exposure to public factors that are lowest during its early life stage. Their finding coincides with Cumming et al. (2019), who found that trading private debt delivers higher returns than simply buying and holding a primary debt issuance. So private debt appears to provide good theoretical grounds to believe that there is alpha. Both the 'special nature' of debt funds, as compared to the traditional bank lending channel and their trading in debt securities appear to make this asset class attractive from a theoretical perspective. The current banking regulation continues to favour private markets, and thus it is plausible that private debt funds will continue to offer alpha opportunities. These funds are thus an example of an alpha candidate.

Continuing with private equity and direct real estate, these assets are not traded and are often smaller in size, making it plausible that they are priced with a discount due to their illiquidity. Additionally, in the case of private equity, a superior form of corporate ownership and governance is assumed to make firms more successful (Jensen, 1989). On the contrary, although not yet supported by empirical evidence, the source of future alpha for 'crypto' assets is thought to reside in new technologies with a projected high future demand.

Factor investing, discretionary investing, and hedge funds seek to implement investment strategies that exploit mispricing within financial markets to generate alpha or, as discussed earlier, they invest in unpopular assets in weak demand. While it is difficult to generate alpha based on mispricing, some hedge funds with relatively low restrictions and high sophistication might plausibly exploit such opportunities. More important than the hypothetical possibility of generating alpha, however, is whether there is credible empirical evidence for such skills.

Empirical Evidence on Alpha

Plausible economic mechanisms that can theoretically generate alpha need to be further tested for their potential to persist after transaction costs and management fees. In addition, the evidence-based investor should ask whether alpha opportunities diminish or even disappear over time as more and more investors seek to exploit them.

In Table 6.1, we summarise selected empirical evidence on alpha from the academic literature. This literature is extensive and reviewing it in great detail falls beyond the scope of our book. Nevertheless, concluding from the research in Table 6.1 we may say that:

Research on private debt suggests that this asset class offers, today, attractive returns as well as alpha against equity and bond portfolios (e.g., Böni & de Roon, 2023; Böni & Manigart, 2023; Cumming et al., 2019). On the other hand, research on private equity has repeatedly shown that private equity has high returns before fees, but is less attractive after fees and when taking into account accurate risk adjustments (e.g., Franzoni et al., 2012; Kaplan & Schoar 2005; Phalippou & Gottschalg, 2008). Direct real estate has also been shown to provide attractive returns in a portfolio context (e.g., Jorda et al. 2019; Kallberg et al., 1996; Martin Hoesli & Witkiewicz 2004). Crypto, with data based on a short sample period only and its high return variance, is difficult to assess. Data limitations and the relatively short history of crypto assets make an evidence-based conclusion about the benefits of holding such assets in a portfolio context difficult (e.g., Harvey et al. 2022). For now, investors must, therefore, rely on their own assessment of this asset class.

We have discussed the empirical performance of factor investing. While several quantitative strategies have been found to perform in empirical studies (e.g., Cooper et al. 2008; Fama & French, 1993, 2015; Hou et al., 2015; Novy-Marx, 2013), factor-investing performance tends to be smaller after the publication of such studies and, after accounting for transaction costs (e.g., Detzel et al., 2023; McLean & Pontiff 2016) the empirical evidence appears to be mixed if taken as a whole. Discretionary investment strategies have been repeatedly shown to underperform, for households as well as professional mutual fund managers (e.g., Barber & Odean 2000; Barber et al. 2008; Fama & French 2010). Hedge funds tend to use more sophisticated strategies and are less constrained, so they should have a better chance of generating alpha. However, after accounting for appropriate risk adjustments, reporting biases in performance figures and relatively high management fees, the empirical evidence on the alpha left to investors is rather modest. The empirical evidence on alpha for this asset class is thus mixed (e.g., Ackermann et al., 1999; Kosowski et al., 2007; Malkiel & Saha 2005).

You may find it disappointing that Table 6.1 does not provide a large list of alpha strategies from which one can 'readily' choose. However, it is not our intention to provide something 'easy' in this respect. Rather, our point is that selecting assets that are likely to generate alpha relative to a global market portfolio is challenging and should be done scientifically, questioning the economic mechanisms at work and studying the empirical evidence available.

References

Ackermann, C., McEnally, R., & Ravenscraft, D. (1999). The performance of hedge funds: Risk, return, and incentives. *Journal of Finance, 54*, 833–874.

Amihud, Y., & Mendelson, H. (1986). Asset pricing and the bid-ask spread. *Journal of Financial Economics, 17*, 223–249.

Barber, B. M., Lee, Y.-T., Liu, Y.-J., & Odean, T. (2008). Just how much do individual investors lose by trading? *Review of Financial Studies, 22*, 609–632.

Barber, B. M., & Odean, T. (2000). Trading is hazardous to your wealth: The common stock investment performance of individual investors. *Journal of Finance, 55*, 773–806.

Block, J., Jang, Y. S., Kaplan, S. N., & Schulze, A. (2023). *A survey of private debt funds* (National Bureau of Economic Research (NBER) working paper no. 30868, pp. 1–65).

Böni, P., & de Roon, F. (2023). Risk-adjusted private debt fund performance and the term structure of alphas. *Social Science Research Network (SSRN)*, 1–66.

Böni, P., & Manigart, S. (2023). Private debt fund returns, persistence, and market conditions. *Financial Analysts Journal, 78*, 121–144.

Chen, X., Wang, J., Wu, C., & Wu, D. (2022). Extreme illiquidity and cross-sectional corporate bond returns. *Review of Financial Studies, 35*, 4902–4947.

Chernenko, S., Erel, I., & Prilmeier, R. (2022). Why do firms borrow directly from nonbanks? *Review of Financial Studies, 35*, 4902–4947.

Cochrane, J. H. (2022). Portfolios for long-term investors. *Review of Finance, 26*, 1–42.

Cooper, M. J., Gulen, H., & Schill, M. J. (2008). Asset growth and the cross-section of stock returns. *Journal of Finance, 63*, 1609–1651.

Cumming, D., Fleming, G., & Liu, Z. (2019). The returns to private debt: Primary issuances vs. secondary acquisitions. *Financial Analysts Journal, 1*, 48–62.

Detzel, A. L., Novy-Marx, R., & Velikov, M. (2023). Model comparison with transaction costs. *Journal of Finance, 78*, 1743–1775.

Fama, E. F. (1993). Common risk factors in the returns on stocks and bonds. *Journal of Financial Economics, 33*, 3–56.

Fama, E. F. (2010). Luck versus skill in the cross section of mutual fund returns. *Journal of Finance, 65*, 1915–1947.

Fama, E. F. (2015). A five-factor asset pricing model. *Journal of Financial Economics, 116*, 1–22.

Franzoni, F., Nowak, E., & Phalippou, L. (2012). Private equity performance and liquidity risk. *Journal of Finance, 67*, 2341–2373.

Harvey, C. R., Abou Zeid, T., Draaisma, T., Luk, M., Neville, H., Rzym, A., & Van Hemert, O. (2022). An investor's guide to crypto. *Journal of Portfolio Management, 49*, 146–171.

Hou, K., Xue, C., & Zhang, L. (2015). Digesting anomalies: An investment approach. *Review of Financial Studies, 28*, 650–705.

Ilmanen, A. (2011). *Expected returns: An investor's guide to harvesting market rewards*. Wiley.

Ilmanen, A. (2022). *Investing amid low expected returns: Making the most when markets offer the least*. Wiley.

Jensen, M. C. (1968). The performance of mutual funds in the period 1945–1964. *Journal of Finance, 23*, 389–416.

Jensen, M. C. (1989). Eclipse of the public corporation. *Harvard Business Review, 67*, 61–74.

Jorda, O., Knoll, K., Kuvshinov, D., Schularick, M., & Taylor, A. (2019). The rate of return on everything 1870–2015. *Quarterly Journal of Economics, 134*, 1225–1298.

Kallberg, J. G., Liu, C. H., & Greig, D. W. (1996). The role of real estate in the portfolio allocation process. *Real Estate Economics, 24*, 359–377.

Kaplan, S. N., & Schoar, A. (2005). Private equity performance: Returns, persistence, and capital flows. *Journal of Finance, 60*, 1791–1823.

Kosowski, R., Naik, N. Y., & Teo, M. (2007). Do hedge funds deliver alpha? A Bayesian and bootstrap analysis. *Journal of Financial Economics, 84*, 229–264.

Malkiel, B. G., & Saha, A. (2005). Hedge funds: Risk and return. *Financial Analysts Journal, 61*, 80–88.

Markowitz, H. (1952). Portfolio selection. *Journal of Finance, 7*, 77–91.

Martin Hoesli, J. L., & Witkiewicz, W. (2004). International evidence on real estate as a portfolio diversifier. *Journal of Real Estate Research, 26*, 161–206.

McLean, R. D., & Pontiff, J. (2016). Does academic research destroy stock return predictability? *Journal of Finance, 71*, 5–32.

Novy-Marx, R. (2013). The other side of value: The gross profitability premium. *Journal of Financial Economics, 108*, 1–28.

Phalippou, L., & Gottschalg, O. (2008). The performance of private equity funds. *Review of Financial Studies, 22*, 1747–1776.

Sharpe, W. F. (1991). The arithmetic of active management. *Financial Analysts Journal, 47*, 7–9.

Singleton, J. C. (2004). *Core-satellite portfolio management: A modern approach for professionally managed funds*. McGraw-Hill.

Treynor, J. L., & Black, F. (1973). How to use security analysis to improve portfolio selection. *Journal of Business, 46*, 66–86.

7

The Risk-Free Investment

The optimal combination of the global market portfolio and the alpha portfolio may result in a portfolio that is too risky for a particular investor. To meet individual risk preferences, investors may invest parts of their total portfolio into risk-free assets. In practice, the concept of a risk-free asset is ambiguous. Accordingly, investors may instead invest in a portfolio of near-risk-free assets, such as money market funds. We consider two types of investors to objectify the subjective term "risk". First, an investor for whom standard deviation is a good measure of risk, and second an investor for whom the probability of loss is important.

Combining the global market portfolio and the alpha portfolio allows investors to find the most efficient portfolio of risky assets with the highest possible Sharpe ratio. However, the absolute risk of this portfolio may be too high for some investors. This is where the risk-free asset comes into place. At first, it sounds counter-intuitive, but the risk-free asset can be used to manage the absolute level of risk across three portfolios. Unlike the expected return on risky assets, the return on the risk-free asset is observable and known (albeit with a few caveats which we shall discuss below). We can, therefore, save ourselves a discussion on how to measure the return of the risk-free asset and how to deal with estimation challenges.

However, we are faced with another problem. There is no single correct measure of risk and investors frequently consider multiple risk measures (see Artzner et al., 1999). As a result, it is often not perfectly clear what risk should be managed. In what follows, we first discuss how the risk-free asset can be

P. Böni and T. Kröncke, *The Evidence-Based Investor*,
https://doi.org/10.1007/978-3-031-88675-1_7

used to manage the most simple measure of risk, namely the expected standard deviation. This measure of risk is often criticised because it measures positive and negative deviations from expected returns symmetrically. A popular alternative are the so-called downside-risk measures, which focus much more on negative deviations from the expected return. While there are many different downside-risk measures available and used in practice, we will have a look at the probability of loss as an exemplary case.

Over an investment horizon of, say, one year, well-diversified multi-asset portfolios have a distribution of returns close to being symmetrical. As a result, the expected standard deviation and the probability of loss are more or less indifferent ways of expressing risk. No matter which measures you use, these measures should provide for a fair assessment of portfolio risk, i.e., they should not lead to a different assessment of the attractiveness of a portfolio.

Things become more interesting, however, as we use a more realistic case for which the investment horizon increases. As we will show, risk as proxied by expected standard deviation differs substantially from risk as proxied by loss probabilities. While the assessment of risk based on the expected standard deviation should not change with a longer investment horizon, it turns out that the probability of loss is likely to decrease as the investment horizon increases. This means that for those investors who are particularly concerned about incurring a loss, a more aggressive portfolio becomes 'less risky' in the long run. So let us dive into this interesting topic of assessing risk.

Managing the Expected Standard Deviation

The expected standard deviation measures the dispersion of realised returns around the expected return. It is commonly referred to as volatility and is a popular measure of risk, presumably due to its simplicity. So far we have focused on this measure of risk, and we start with this measure before we shed light on an alternative measure.

Figure 7.1 shows a hypothetical example of a combined efficient portfolio. The efficient portfolio (blue) is a combination of 70% of the market sub-portfolio (green), 30% of the alpha sub-portfolio (red), and 0% of the portfolio holding the risk-free assets. This combined efficient portfolio, comprising three sub-portfolios has a standard deviation of 10%. It turns out that the risk can be halved to a standard deviation of 5% by investing 50% in the efficient portfolio (blue) and 50% in the risk-free asset (grey). Investing 50% in the efficient portfolio simply means that we have to invest 35% in the market sub-portfolio and 15% in the alpha portfolio. Of course, the expected return is also reduced proportionally. Importantly, the Sharpe ratio of the portfolio remains unchanged, as all portfolios on the line connecting the risk-free asset and the efficient portfolio have the same Sharpe ratio.

As Fig. 7.1 shows, it is relatively easy to reduce the overall portfolio risk by adding the risk-free asset while simultaneously reducing the weight in the efficient portfolio (which consists of the global market portfolio and the alpha portfolio). The question is then how much risk a specific investor should be prepared to take.

Expected utility theory, as developed by Neumann and Morgenstern (1953), provides an answer to this question. The basic idea is that investors balance the positive utility they receive from the expected return and the negative utility from the expected risk. The balancing parameter is termed 'risk aversion'. Investors with high-risk aversion want to pick a low-risk portfolio, for example, with a standard deviation of 5%. On the other hand, investors with low-risk aversion prefer a high-risk portfolio, for example, one with a standard deviation of 10%.

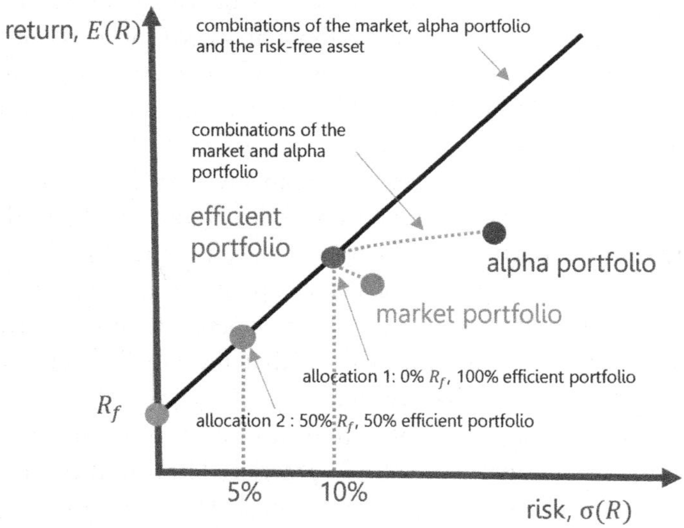

Fig. 7.1 Using the risk-free asset to manage risk This figure illustrates how the risk-free asset is used to manage the risk of the portfolio. Allocation 1 invests 100% in the efficient portfolio and 0% in the risk-free asset. Allocation 2 invests 50% in the efficient portfolio and 50% in the risk-free asset. As a result, Allocation 2 has half the risk of Allocation 1. Both allocations still have the highest possible Sharpe ratio, as indicated by the slope of the black line. Own illustration

In general, the optimal share of the risky asset depends on the functional form of how investors balance return and risk. However, as shown in Campbell and Viceira (2017), there is a simple approximate solution under quite general conditions:

$$W = \frac{1}{\gamma} \times \frac{\mathbb{E}[R_t] - R_f}{\sigma(R_t)^2},$$

where W is the share of total assets invested in the efficient portfolio, $1 - W$ is the share invested in the risk-free asset, and γ is the relative risk aversion. Typical risk aversion levels lie between one (indicating very low-risk aversion) and ten (very high-risk aversion).[1] Note that the second fraction is not the Sharpe ratio, but rather the excess return of the efficient portfolio divided by the squared standard deviation instead of the simple standard deviation.

Imagine a very risk-averse person who chooses from different portfolios. If the excess return of the efficient portfolio is 4% and the standard deviation is 10%, then an investor with high-risk aversion (and $\gamma = 8$) will choose an optimal allocation to sub-portfolios with $W = 50\%$. This would be Allocation 2 in Fig. 7.1. On the other hand, an investor who is not particularly risk averse, as proxied by $\gamma = 4$, should choose an allocation with $W = 100\%$, which is Allocation 1 in Fig. 7.1. We see that there are two key investment decisions that investors need to make to find an optimal allocation among three distinct portfolios.

The first decision is how much capital an investor should allocate to the alpha portfolio and the global market portfolio. Figure 7.1 shows this unique combination of two portfolios, which together form the efficient portfolio.

The second decision is how to allocate capital between the efficient portfolio of risky assets and the risk-free asset to obtain the final portfolio. The aim here is to adjust the absolute risk so that the portfolio aligns with the investor's appetite for risk (risk aversion).

While this sounds easy in theory, we next discuss three important hurdles in determining the risk of a portfolio in practice. These hurdles are related to (i) considering the investment horizon when defining the risk-free asset, (ii)

[1] Empirical evidence provided by Giglio et al. (2021) suggests that the risk-taking of investors qualitatively aligns with this simple approximate solution presented. However, the fit is quantitatively not great and other factors, such as gender, age, and the financial situation of investors should also be considered when assessing risk aversion. Moreover, recent empirical studies provide evidence that loss aversion could also be considered when assessing investor preferences. Van Dolder and Vandenbroucke (2024), for example, find that female, older, and less well-off participants are more risk averse than male, younger, and more well-off participants, and that loss aversion and risk aversion are distinct concepts that serve complementary roles in capturing investor preferences. Adding loss aversion to our example is beyond the scope of our book, however.

considering the time variation of risk (in the short and the long run), and (iii) considering additional potential constraints on the downside risk.

Investment Horizon. First, as pointed out by Campbell and Viceira (2001, 2002), what the selected risk-free asset is to be depends on the investment horizon of the investor. For example, an investor with a one-year horizon should consider the risk-free rate for an asset with a maturity of one year. Likewise, an investor with a 10-year horizon should base decisions on the risk-free rate for an asset with a maturity of ten years. Long-term investors might be confronted with yet another challenge. A truly risk-free asset should guarantee a real amount of value at the end of the investment horizon and not simply a nominal amount. However, nominal amounts often do not reflect the true amounts, due to inflation. To the extent that inflation is unexpected and, therefore, not reflected in the yield of a risk-free asset, the risk-free rate will not fully reflect an asset's true risk. Inflation-linked risk-free bonds may however provide a solution to this challenge. Yes, they have been increasingly available in recent years, although their availability for assets with different maturities is still limited. Even if available, due to the relatively small market for inflation-linked bonds, they are likely to carry an illiquidity premium (Ermolov, 2021). A truly risk-free asset is thus hard to find. This challenge is smaller for the short-term investor, as short-term risk-free bonds adjust quickly to changes in expected inflation as they are frequently rolled over. A long-term investor may, therefore, wish to roll over a short-term bond or an investment that is closer to cash. While theoretically better, finding and investing in long-term inflation-linked bonds is more challenging.[2]

Time Variation of Risk. Second, risk, or rather the expected standard deviation, varies over time. In the academic literature, this time variation is known as volatility clustering. It is often observed in times of crisis and characterised by a rising standard deviation following a large drop in the stock market, the first often remaining elevated thereafter (Kroencke, 2022 for an empirical investigation). This makes the analysis and especially the forecasting of volatility challenging to the financial economist and investor alike. The seminal ARCH/GARCH models developed by Engle (1982) and Bollerslev (1986) have helped us to overcome the challenges related to modelling

[2] We admit that such a short-term risk-free asset is not completely risk-free for investors with a long investment horizon. For example, if real interest rates fall, the long-term investor using short-term bonds for risk management would roll into lower and lower real interest rates over time—reflecting reinvestment risk Campbell and Viceira (2001). Long-term studies of capital market returns (e.g., Ibbotson et al., 1985; Jorda et al., 2019) suggest that real interest rates are modest over time, and in this light, the roll-over risk is usually limited.

time variation in volatility.[3] Nevertheless, volatility clustering is an important property of financial data that investors with a relatively short investment horizon (e.g., over one day or a few weeks) should consider. It should however be less relevant for long-term investors, as volatility tends to return to its long-term value (i.e., it reverts to the mean within a few months after a spike). Rather than considering volatility clustering, long-term investors should contemplate the relevance of structural changes in long-term volatility. Such structural shifts in volatility are less often discussed in the literature and yet they are well documented statistically and can have important ramifications for the optimal share of the efficient portfolio. For example, US stocks were much more volatile between 1929 and 1939 than afterwards (Schwert, 1989). It is however difficult to distinguish structural shifts from more temporary increases in volatility (clustering) in real time. However, studying long-term capital market expectations, as discussed above, can help investors identify structural shifts across asset classes.

Measures of Downside Risk. Third, another issue with the standard deviation is that it measures deviations from the expected return symmetrically. So, a 5% return above the expected return is as bad as a 5% return below the expected return. For many investors, this property is counter-intuitive. As a response, several so-called downside-risk measures have been proposed in the literature. These have the explicit goal of better capturing the risk of losses. Typically, measures of downside risk are not used in isolation, but rather as additional constraints on the optimal share of the efficient risky-asset portfolio (W).[4]

Managing risk can thus be achieved by combining the efficient portfolio (which comprises the global market portfolio and the alpha portfolio) with the risk-free asset. An investor's risk aversion drives the decision of how much capital should be allocated to the efficient portfolio (W), and how much to the risk-free asset ($1 - W$).

Using volatility, as proxied by the standard deviation of returns, to estimate risk, is common. However, investors might also consider the probability of loss as a downside-risk measure. As you will see in the following section, this measure is both popular and intuitive.

---

[3] ARCH and GARCH models stand for autoregressive conditional heteroskedasticity and generalised autoregressive conditional heteroskedasticity. They are designed to deal with volatility clustering. See Engle (2001) for a summary with an illustration of popular applications.

[4] A discussion of the differences and properties of such downside-risk measures is provided in Artzner et al. (1999).

Managing the Probability of a Loss

The probability of a loss captures the likelihood of losing money over a given investment horizon. Generally speaking, the strength of this measure is that it is easy to imagine what it captures. For example, almost any investor will agree that the lower the probability of loss, the better. An important shortcoming is that it does not capture how much money is lost in the event of a loss. We will come back to this point later.

Estimating the probability of a loss requires measuring the left tail of the distribution of a portfolio return, which is typically done using historical data or by making a distributional assumption. At the annual time horizon, a diversified multi-asset portfolio is relatively well approximated by a log-normal distribution (Campbell et al., 1997). This means that the standard deviation of such a portfolio can be used to obtain a first approximation of a realistic probability of a loss.

For example, let us assume that the efficient portfolio offers an expected return of 6% and the risk-free asset only 1%. With a standard deviation of 10%, the probability of a loss at the one-year horizon is 29.1%.[5] One would expect to observe a loss about every three years due to the relatively wide distribution of returns around the expected value. For Allocation 2 shown in Fig. 7.1, which invests 50% in the risk-free asset, the expected return and standard deviation are reduced to 3.5% and 5%, respectively. The according probability of a loss is then 25% at the annual horizon,[6] and we should observe a loss every four years.

When historical data are available, it can be feasible to use bootstrap methods as in Fama and French (2018), Anarkulova et al. (2022) to avoid the log-normal assumption. Capital market assumptions can be used to shift the mean of the historical data or scale the return dispersion to account for current developments and a forward-looking assessment of the available investment opportunities.

If the standard deviation allows us to find (albeit only approximately) the probability of a loss, then why is using the standard deviation alone insufficient? One reason is that both measures behave differently as the investment horizon is increased. If portfolio returns are approximately independent from

[5] The assumption is that the log-return is approximately normally distributed. Then we can find the probability of a loss from the z-score $(0 - [0.06 - 0.5 \times 0.10^2])/0.10 = -0.55$. The adjustment in the numerator converts the simple expected return to the approximate logarithm of the expected return. The z-score is standard normal distributed. Finally, a statistical table showing the cumulative distribution function of the standard normal distribution allows us to find the probability of a loss of 29.1%.

[6] We can find the probability from the z-score $(0 - [0.035 - 0.5 \times 0.05^2])/0.05 = -0.675$.

one year to the next, then the variance scales with the investment horizon. The share of the efficient portfolio (W), which depends on the variance, remains unchanged with an increasing investment horizon, and the split between the risk-free asset and the efficient portfolio is the same for all investment horizons.

However, with an increasing investment horizon, the probability of a loss is different. With a positive geometric return, the probability of a loss declines as the investment horizon expands. This is because the portfolio value is expected to shift upwards over time and away from the loss hurdle. In our example, based on Fig. 7.1, Allocation 1 has a probability of a loss after ten years of 4.1%, while Allocation 2 has a probability of a loss after ten years of less than 1.6%. Investors concerned about the probability of loss should be less so as the investment horizon expands. For that reason, providing investors with long-horizon simulations of the potential return distribution, and particularly long-term downside-risk measures, can be crucial when deciding the optimal split between the risk-free asset, the global market portfolio, and the alpha portfolio.

Let us take a look at a simulation of the long-horizon returns for the evidence-based global market portfolio (as determined in Table 5.1, above) in Fig. 7.2, and the distribution of ten-year returns for the same portfolio in Fig. 7.3. Our simulation is based on the median values of a set of institutional capital market assumptions we have collected.

Figure 7.2 shows the percentage of simulated long-horizon returns of an investment of one Swiss Franc within a certain interval for different investment horizons. Clearly, the distribution becomes wider over time as the expected standard deviation increases with the horizon. The horizontal dotted line corresponds to a value of one Swiss Franc. The area below the dotted line is the simulation where the investor observes a loss in her portfolio. As anticipated, the area below the dotted line shrinks with an increasing investment horizon.

Next, we add to our simulation in Fig. 7.3, which shows the distribution across simulations for an investment horizon of ten years. The simulation outcome is now on the x-axis, and the percentage of simulations is the area below the curve. About 6.6% of the simulations result in a portfolio value of less than 1 Swiss franc after ten years (i.e., corresponding to an investment loss). The median outcome after ten years is 1.58 Swiss francs (i.e., a return of 58% on the initial investment). In the 5% of the best simulations, the portfolio outcome is above 2.6, corresponding to a return of 160% or more. Importantly, investors can effectively manage the downside risk as captured by the probability of loss. Investing 60% in the global market portfolio and

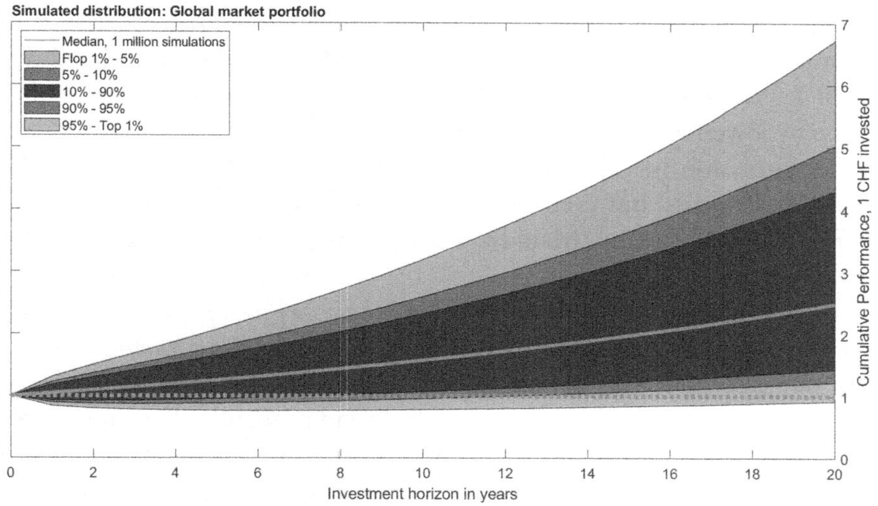

Fig. 7.2 Simulation of long-horizon Swiss Franc returns for the global market portfolio. This figure reports the expected distribution of one million simulations of the global market portfolio from the one-year mark to the 20-year investment horizon. The expected return and risk are based on institutional capital market assumptions as reported in Table 5.1. The expected return for the portfolio is 5.01% p.a. and the expected standard deviation is 10.09% p.a.. *Source* Own calculations

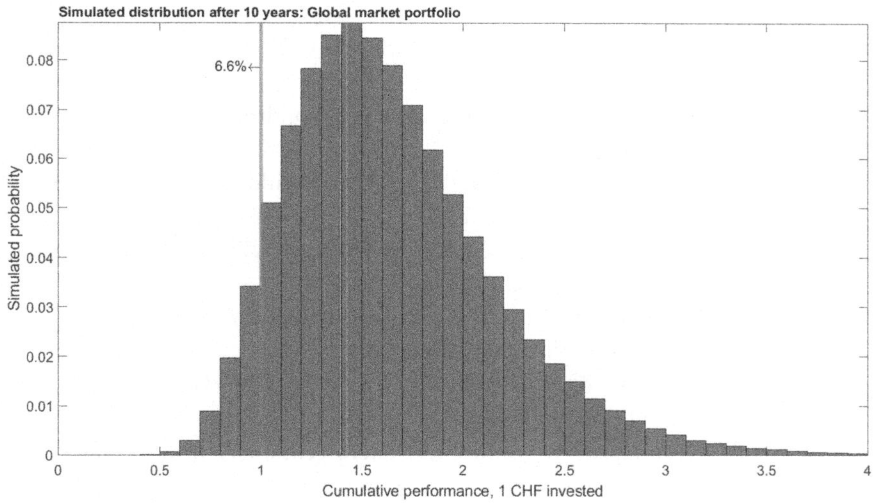

Fig. 7.3 Distribution of ten-year returns for the evidence-based global market portfolio. This figure shows our simulation of the long-horizon return distribution for the evidence-based global market portfolio as determined in Table 5.1. It is based on median values of a broad sample of institutional capital market assumptions. The simulation outcome is shown on the x-axis, the percentage of simulations is shown by the area under the curve. *Source* own calculations

40% in the risk-free asset would reduce the probability of loss to 3.5% at the ten-year horizon. A 40%/60% portfolio would come with a probability of loss of 1.5%. Of course, in exchange, the investor has to give up some of the upside by lowering their expected return.

The discussion in this chapter illustrates a principle that is relevant not only to economists, but even more so to investors: '*the principle that there is no free lunch*'. As Gregory Mankiw, a macroeconomist at Harvard University, puts it:

"*To get one thing that we like, we usually have to give up another thing that we like. Making decisions requires trading off one goal against another.*"

In our case, investors must trade off risk against expected return. As we have shown, this should be done consciously and prudently. The most important thing is not to give up return and/or increase risk unconsciously, by falling for one of the investment myths that we lay bare in this book.

References

Anarkulova, A., Cederburg, S., & O'Doherty, M. S. (2022). Stocks for the long run? evidence from a broad sample of developed markets. *Journal of Financial Economics, 143*, 409–33.

Artzner, P., Delbaen, F., Eber, J.-M., & Heath, D. (1999). Coherent measures of risk. *Mathematical Finance, 9*, 203–28.

Bollerslev, T. (1986). Generalized autoregressive conditional heteroskedasticity. *Journal of Econometrics, 31*, 307–27.

Campbell, J. Y., & Viceira, L. M. (2001). Who should buy long-term bonds? *Amercian Economic Review, 91*, 99–127.

Campbell, J. Y., & Viceira, L. M. (2002). *Strategic asset allocation: Portfolio choice for long-term investors*. Oxford University Press.

Campbell, J. Y., & Viceira, L. M. (2017). *Financial decisions and markets: A course in asset pricing*. Princeton University Press.

Campbell, J. Y., Lo, A. W., & MacKinlay, A. C. (1997). *The econometrics of financial markets*. Princeton University Press.

Engle, R. (1982). Autoregressive conditional heteroscedasticity with estimates of the variance of united kingdom inflation. *Econometrica, 50*, 987–1007.

Engle, R. (2001). Garch 101: The use of arch/garch models in applied econometrics. *Journal of Economic Perspectives, 15*, 157–68.

Ermolov, A. (2021). When and where is it cheaper to issue inflation-linked debt? *Review of Asset Pricing Studies, 11*, 610–53.

Fama, E. F., & French, K. R. (2018). Long-horizon returns. *Review of Asset Pricing Studies, 8*, 232–52.

Giglio, S., Maggiori, M., Stroebel, J., & Utkus, S. (2021). Five facts about beliefs and portfolios. *American Economic Review, 111*, 1481–522.
Ibbotson, R. G., Siegel, L. B., & Lovel, K. S. (1985). World wealth: Market values and returns. *Journal of Portfolio Management, 12*, 4–23.
Jorda, O., Knoll, K., Kuvshinov, D., Schularick, M., & Taylor, A. (2019). The rate of return on everything 1870–2015. *Quarterly Journal of Economics, 134*, 1225–98.
Kroencke, T. A. (2022). Recessions and the stock market. *Journal of Monetary Economics, 131*, 61–77.
Schwert, G. W. (1989). Why does stock market volatility change over time? *Journal of Finance, 44*, 1115–53.
Van Dolder, D., & Vandenbroucke, J. (2024). Behavioral risk profiling: Measuring loss aversion of individual investors. *Journal of Banking and Finance* forthcoming, 511–535.
Von Neumann, J., & Morgenstern, O. (1953). *Theory of games and economic behavior*. Princeton University Press.

8

Mastering Investment Myths: A Recapitulation

This chapter summarises the key messages of the book. In particular, it examines the pitfalls of common investment myths and how an evidence-based approach based on a 3-portfolio strategy can help investors overcome them.

Congratulations on your successful navigation through the complexities and nuanced insights presented in this book. Your commitment to deepening your understanding of the intricate dynamics that shape the discipline of investing is commendable, and this achievement will undoubtedly enhance your analytical acumen within the domain of investment management.

In contrast to the typical investor, as documented in academic research, you should now be able to consciously avoid falling for the investment myths we have laid bare in this book. You are now unlikely to sacrifice returns or take unnecessary risks, and you are thus enabled to achieve your long-term investment goals.

In the next section, we briefly summarise the ten investment myths and how they can be overcome. Finally, we will consciously revisit the three-portfolio strategy we have devised to help you successfully achieve long-term capital appreciation.

P. Böni and T. Kröncke, *The Evidence-Based Investor*,
https://doi.org/10.1007/978-3-031-88675-1_8

Conquering the Ten Investment Myths

Conquering the Market-Participation Myth: A simple global market portfolio has historically delivered annual returns of approximately 6%, a figure that remains plausible for future long-term performance. Despite this, only 49% of US households, and significantly fewer in Switzerland (31%), Germany (23%), and Austria (9%), participate in equity markets. Consequently, a large proportion of households forgo potential long-term capital appreciation. To achieve returns comparable to a diversified global market portfolio, investors need to participate in capital markets. But what if a global market portfolio seems too risky for a particular investor? The 3-portfolio strategy outlined in this book makes it possible to tailor the overall risk of a portfolio to a specific investor's risk preference, making such concerns unwarranted.

Conquering the Investment-Concentration Myth: Many investors tend to prioritise returns over risk, leading to under-diversified portfolios. Yet many single stocks end with a loss at the end of their lifetime, and most thus underperform the risk-free rate. Under-diversified portfolios resemble lottery betting. A passive, diversified portfolio may seem less thrilling, but it significantly improves the likelihood of positive long-term returns. For this very reason, a well-diversified global market portfolio is at the heart of the 3-portfolio strategy.

Conquering the Stock Picking Myth: Non-professional investors usually fail to outperform passive investment strategies after taking into account transaction costs. Thus, stock picking is unlikely to generate significant outperformance over a long horizon.

Conquering the Active-Investing Myth: Professionals do somewhat better than retail investors. They manage to outperform the market somewhat before deducting fees. However, after fees, little to nothing is usually left for investors. A portfolio that invests to a large extent passively in different markets can significantly reduce cost, thereby directly increasing performance.

Conquering the Home-Bias Myth: Investors tend to overweight domestic assets, neglecting the diversification benefits of an internationally diversified portfolio, despite accrued evidence that it has done so since the 1970s. Even institutional investors frequently overlook this advantage. To counter any domestic bias against foreign investments, investors can, for example, draw on the capital market assumptions of institutional asset managers and consultants. They show that Nestle, Novartis, and Roche are not the only good investments on the planet. Of course, the 3-portfolio strategy includes a global market portfolio and not just a local market portfolio.

Conquering the Market-Timing Myth: Investors often try to time the market, using trend signals, dividend yields (and related fundamental ratios,) term spreads, other bond yields and spreads, volatility, corporate reports, and economic activity. The academic literature finds that predicting returns is easy in hindsight, yet fails in real time. Researchers have still not identified those factors which reliably predict stock returns out-of-sample! The 3-portfolio strategy thus steers clear of market-timing strategies.

Conquering the Factor-Investing Myth: Investors often attempt to predict stock returns using firm-specific factors such as size, value, momentum, investment, profitability, and beta. Historical performance metrics in academic studies are indeed impressive. However, the real-world performance of factor strategies is worse and often mixed at best. Performance decay after publication has been documented and, on top of this, one has to account for transaction costs, brokerage fees, and commissions. Factor strategies belong on the list of candidates for the alpha portfolio. However, qualifying for the alpha portfolio is challenging. To be included requires a plausible economic mechanism and convincing empirical evidence that the factor strategy helps (net of all costs) to improve the performance of the global market portfolio.

Conquer the Performance-Persistence Myth: Choosing investments based on past short-term performance is extremely popular, though scientifically unfounded and constitutes bad investment advice. Judging an investment by its short-term past performance does not help us to find better investments. The academic literature overwhelmingly finds that past performance, after carefully adjusting for risk, does not persist into the future. There is no evidence for the existence of skilled or informed portfolio managers whose acumen translates into performance persistence. The 3-portfolio strategy thus does not make any investment decisions based on past short-term performance.

Conquering the Volatility-Irrelevance Myth: More volatile investment strategies are likely to top short-term performance rankings due to luck rather than good judgement. Investors who systematically choose highly ranked investments are likely to pick those investments that come with higher volatility without higher return potential. However, uncompensated volatility is a drag on long-term performance. The expected Sharpe ratio, as a preferred investment criterion, avoids this problem and is therefore what the 3-portfolio strategy aims to maximise.

Conquering the ESG-Investing Myth: While popular, ESG stocks or funds are expected to underperform the market in the long term when taking a basic demand and supply argument into account. This is partially due to investors conceding returns for doing the right thing. Furthermore, from an economist's standpoint, other tools would likely do more good for the same amount of performance conceded. Investors may however still have such strong preferences for ESG that they are willing to accept these costs. The global market portfolio can then be adapted to meet such a constraint using exclusion or best-in-class ESG restrictions. Indeed, a fourth portfolio, the impact investing portfolio, could complement the three-portfolio approach, as it is separated from the other investments and can be evaluated by its realised versus expected impact on E, S, or G. Investors can then stick to the principle of using different sub-portfolios to achieve divergent goals.

Mastering Thousands of Investment Opportunities Using the Simple 3-Portfolio Strategy

The 3-portfolio strategy outlined in this book not only allows investors to overcome the 10 investment myths we expose as Siren song, but also to deal selectively with thousands of available investments. The beauty is that each of the three portfolios has its own specific objective against which it can be continually evaluated within a scientific, evidence-based approach. In the following, we summarise the most important key aspects.

Portfolio 1—The Global Market Portfolio to Build the Foundation: This portfolio aims to lay the foundation for the composite portfolio. Firstly, this is achieved by diversifying across asset classes (equities, bonds, and liquid real assets) and investing globally (across the US, Europe, Asia Pacific, and Emerging Markets). Second, we argue that the global market portfolio is best implemented through passive, low-cost investment vehicles such as ETFs. The global market portfolio will achieve a fair risk/return trade-off, which already puts it ahead of most investors' portfolios.

The question then arises of how best to blend different asset classes. We do not recommend discretionary approaches, which are probably the most common approach currently in practice. Such portfolios tend to suffer from the emotions and gut feelings of a few persons in charge, often leading to poor performance. While value weighting works within, for example, the equity market, a value-weighted global multi-asset portfolio would be very bond-heavy. For this reason, we do not recommend this approach either. A fixed-weight multi-asset portfolio is another emotion-free alternative, although it does not take into account political or fundamental developments that may be of relevance to financial markets. This approach is all too often not an option, especially for investors with a fiduciary duty to fulfil.

This book offers a novel alternative to the dilemma. Recent academic research suggests that consensus institutional capital market assumptions are consistent with finance theory and are thus informative about the relative attractiveness of asset classes. We have illustrated how to construct a rule-based global market portfolio, one which is guided by such institutional capital market assumptions. It combines the best aspects of discretionary and fixed weights approaches and avoids their respective downsides. Our proposed approach is rule-based (as opposed to discretionary) and evidence-based, as political or fundamental developments reflected in institutional capital market assumptions will be also reflected in the multi-asset allocation.

Portfolio 2—The Alpha Portfolio: Enhancing Expected Performance: The global market portfolio is likely to have an attractive expected Sharpe ratio, yet is unlikely to offer the *best possible* expected Sharpe ratio. This is not a contradiction, but rather reflects the picture that academic studies paint of modern capital markets.

Investors wishing to further enhance the performance of their portfolio should consider allocating a portion of their assets to alpha opportunities. Such alpha opportunities are aggregated within the alpha portfolio, and the investor then combines the global market portfolio with this alpha portfolio. The global market portfolio is necessary to identify alpha opportunities and thus serves as a benchmark and hurdle that candidates for the alpha portfolio must pass. We have emphasised that there should be a reasonable economic mechanism that makes it plausible that the alpha candidate contributes to outperformance, as well as convincing empirical evidence.

Now, this step is time-consuming and can be expensive. Some investors may conclude that the global market portfolio is good enough and drop the alpha portfolio from their investment menu altogether. Other investors may focus on a few very promising alpha opportunities in order to maintain efficiency in the investment process. A few, probably large investors, might consider a broad search for alpha opportunities. There may also be strong investor-specific preferences for certain types of alpha opportunities, such as less liquid private market investments or trading strategies in liquid markets. So while the global market portfolio may be identical, or at least very similar, for a wide range of investors, the alpha portfolio is generally individual and investor-specific.

Portfolio 3—Using Risk-Free Assets to Manage Risk: The global market portfolio (portfolio one) and the alpha portfolio (portfolio two) are combined so as to maximise the expected Sharpe ratio. However, the absolute amount of risk of this combined portfolio can be too large for a given investor.

The good news is that we do not need complex derivatives or costly trading strategies to fix the problem. Instead, investors allocate a certain fraction in the risk-free asset until the overall risk of the three portfolios meets their risk preferences.

The bad news is that there are some practical obstacles to overcome. Unfortunately, risk is notoriously ambiguous. For some investors, volatility adequately captures risk while, for others, downside risk may be more relevant. Depending on the measure of risk employed, the investment horizon may or may not be important. Choices have to be made about which measure of risk to choose and how to balance multiple measures. In many cases, the risk-free asset will be sufficient to find a balance and manage the overall risk of the portfolio. Finally, investors will rarely find a truly risk-free asset on the investment menu list available to them. Typically, a portfolio of near-risk-free assets will be used as a pragmatic solution.

Odysseus successfully overcame the deadly temptation of the Sirens, mythical creatures whose enchanting songs lured sailors to their doom, causing their ships to run aground on rocky shores. Like Odysseus, you are now aware of the dangers of the ten investment myths. Like Odysseus, you are now well-equipped to hear the Siren song of the financial advisor without falling victim to it. Like Odysseus, you have taken the necessary precautions to hear their song without paying heed to it, thereby overcoming the danger they pose.

Your investment success is a triumph of intellect and self-discipline, as you are now able to develop an investment strategy that allows you to safely navigate the perilous challenges of investing without losing control or jeopardising your wealth.

Index

P. Böni and T. Kröncke, *The Evidence-Based Investor*,
https://doi.org/10.1007/978-3-031-88675-1

The manufacturer's authorised representative in the EU is Springer Nature Customer Service Centre GmbH, Europaplatz 3, 69115 Heidelberg, Germany. If you have any concerns regarding our products, please contact ProductSafety@springernature.com

Printed and bound by CPI Group (UK) Ltd, Croydon, CR0 4YY
30/09/2026
02225514-0020